The Journey Goes On

ISBN 978-0-9561554-0-5

PORTBANK
·PRINTWORKS·

Published By Portbank Printworks 2009

Men With Pens

Published by Portbank Printworks 2009

Foreword

So much has happened since I first met the Men with Pens, six years ago. A few more grey hairs or pink scalp; a few pounds here or there in weight; a scar, perhaps, or wounds that don't show.

The group called Men with Pens has morphed a little round the edges. There have been some new infusions of fresh blood and there has been a significant loss, too. Yet through it all, the body that is Men with Pens is hale and hearty, still going strong.

Guest tutors have introduced new exercises into their regime but it's the Men themselves who do the work that keeps the writing supple. This year there have been trips to the Edinburgh Book Festival and to Wigtown Booktown. Closer to home there have been readings as part of North Lanarkshire Council's 'Words 2008' festival of the written word. The Men with Pens are keen participants. Pushing themselves. Stretching. Growing.

This is the latest collection of their writing and art work. It's wholesome and nourishing fare to feed body, mind and spirit. Tuck in!

Carol McKay, former tutor.

www.carolmckay.co.uk

Contents

REGINALD SCOTT THOMPSON

1934 – 2007

-A REQUIEM-

This year, in the sixth year of the founding of The Men with Pens, we are saddened by the sudden passing of Reg Thompson; one of the stalwarts of our group. I first met Reg, as he was known, at Coatbridge Library writing group.

We found we had much in common both being ex-servicemen – Reg in the Navy and myself in the RAF. We struck up an instant rapport which culminated in an enduring friendship. We shared many interests, including chess, a love of art and history, and, of course, writing. We both joined together when we met up with the original founders of The Men with Pens; Rab, Jim and Jim Graham, in the autumn of 2001.

Although we had differing views of the world at large and had many heated debates we respected each other's views. Reg was a great inspiration to me personally and was also a marvellous supporter of the work of the group members, always showing a keen interest in all that was produced.

Reg was one of that rare breed, a self-taught man who believed sincerely in helping others and sharing his varied talents. He had worked at various occupations and had vast experience of life which can be seen in his writings.

We have dedicated this latest volume to his everlasting memory. A memory which we all hold dear in our hearts. Reg was a fighter. Even when ill he still strove to attend group meetings and was our very first Chairman after we developed our constitution.

In this volume you will find fine examples of his prose and poetry . The best tribute to Reg however, is the poem entitled simply 'Reg' by writer Rab Higgins in this collection. A fitting memorial to a great friend, writer and man.

I.N.R. Johnston

This is a collection of writing by,

Reg Thompson

Published by Portbank Printworks 2009

Holding On

She holds him tight,
they walk hand in hand
The sea breeze blows
across their sadness.
How much time is left,
he was almost gone.
In this uncertainty,
she tries to hold on.

Adjustment so hard
in the simplest task.
To rekindle the past
a dream built on sand.
Back to her memories
of his time now gone.
His lifetime of toil
recedes with the tide.

She holds his hand
he gazes at the sea.
Minutes pass by, she
points across the bay.
Vacant eyes and mind
trying hard to adjust.
She turns him round,
leaves a memory behind.

Harmony with Nature

His affinity with humans
is known far and wide.
This solitary creature
feels safe by your side.
Appearing out of nowhere
he darts round your feet,
keeping his distance.
Yet still takes his seat.

He perches just waiting
on the rake or the hoe.
His brown eye watching
for the titbit to show.
It is strange as you work
how your senses are aware.
Though you don't see him,
you still know he is there.

To appreciate the beauty
as in nature's great plan.
The lonely little robin
is in harmony with man.
What a comfort and joy
from beginning to the end,
such pleasure to work with
my red-breasted friend.

Nothing is Perfect

Leaning heavily on his silver-handled cane James Trethowan walked slowly along the leaf-strewn avenue. He took a deep breath of the cold crisp autumn air. His shuffling gait through the brown dry leaves was the only sound to be heard. Ten minutes earlier he had left his luxurious hotel in the centre of town. The taxi driver had dropped him off at the bottom of the road.

Forty years ago he had left England in some haste. Now he was back in the land where he was born. Had his journey back home begun by fate? On the Paris Metro someone had left a magazine lying on the seat beside him. James Trethowan had picked it up and was browsing through it when he was drawn to a brightly coloured advert. Gazing intently at the picturesque scene, he was amazed to see it was a small glossy painting of his former home. Meticulously he had studied the small print reading carefully each line of the fine details.

'Eighteenth-century stone-built cottage with thatched roof for sale on the outskirts of Chester. All modern facilities fitted throughout, designed to blend in with the Victorian style furniture and fittings. Situated in an acre of mature gardens. Once belonged to famous landscape artist and author. For further details: Contact Estate Agents, Howard and Sedgley, Clarence Street, Chester.'

When he had arrived home he had immediately contacted the estate agents. An appointment was made for the following morning.

Travel arrangements and hotel accommodation were booked for that evening. The next morning he had met a young estate agent, Clarrisa Howard, in her office. He had insisted he would make his own way there to view the cottage. Now here he was only a short walk away from his former home.

Turning right at the end of the leafy avenue, he stopped to gaze over the top of the hawthorn hedge. Taking a deep breath, he thought after all this time nothing here had changed. The huge expanse of mature woodland stretched out before him. Staring into the cold stillness, James Trethowan believed, after what had happened here, life would never be the same. Yet here he was back after all these years. Was this destiny?

Struggling on, he came to a sharp bend in the road. There it was, everything as he had remembered it. He stood gazing at it trying to connect with his past. The cottage looked much the same to him as it had done in those dark days. This was not the end of the road, for him it was the beginning of a pilgrimage. Beside the gate was a silver-grey 2000 Frontera. He walked slowly up the path and tapped on the solid oak door with his stick.

Heavy footsteps echoed on the floorboards, disturbing the peace of the quiet autumn morning. The door was opened by the young estate agent Clarrisa Howard whom he had met the previous day. He noticed her heavy boots which accounted for the noise. Designer cords, woolly jumper and fur-lined casual fitted in well with her Frontera. Observation to detail was an important part of his profession. On the first day he had met her, memories from his distant past had been rekindled.

"Good morning Mr Trethowan, I didn't see you arrive, come in."

"I'm just here this minute."

"Did you enjoy your walk?"

"Yes very much, I wanted to see the surrounding area."

"The countryside is lovely here at this time of year."

"Tell me Miss Howard, when was the road blocked off out there?"

"As far as I know the road had always stopped just beyond this cottage." He thought, she's probably too young to remember.

"Would you like a cup of tea before I show you round?"

"That's very kind of you, but it won't be necessary to give me a guided tour." Clarrisa Howard was surprised by his remark, has he changed his mind? She thought something must have spooked him. He seemed anxious now about the road being blocked off.

"We have a number of other desirable properties in this area if this is unsuitable Mr Trethowan?"

"On the contrary Miss Howard, you have mistaken my intentions. I believe it was offers over £150,000?"

"Yes, I'm sorry I misunderstood. I thought maybe you had lost interest".

"Not at all, but I don't wish to get involved in an auction. My offer is £200,000. You have my number, contact me at my hotel." The young estate agent was completely taken aback. She was aware none of the other bids were in any way comparable. Delighted the way things had turned out, she offered him a lift back to his hotel. James Trethowan politely declined and set off towards the town. There was something he had to do. James Trethowan had much on his mind.

Walking slowly back along the tree-lined avenue, he wondered if any of the wealthy families he had known still lived here. Would they remember me, would they know anything about me now? One place he wanted to go was the old library. He remembered it used to be situated on the corner of Windsor Square. He was pleased to see the façade of the old Victorian buildings on the streets had been restored. Probably mass consumerism is hidden inside he thought. Not that it mattered to James Trethowan, who had lived a spartan existence as a writer in Paris for years. Shunning fame he had given the bulk of his considerable fortune to medical research.

Later he arrived at the place where he had spent hours studying. The solid oak doors, the sculptured intricate stonework was his England. The atmosphere inside engulfed him, this was where he belonged. He gazed round at the thousands of books on the shelves. Sitting down in the small reading area, he thought about works of the old masters. How the words of these ghosts of the past had shaped his life.

Lifting some books at random from one of the shelves, he scanned a few pages. Some were not to his liking but he didn't dismiss them. James

Trethowan thought about the seed, where had it all begun? The long lonely hours, the discipline, had fame or perfection been their motivation?

Wandering through to the poetry section, he glanced at some of the books; Shelley and Byron were his favourites. Where had the seed for their ideas come from? Did they use real situations to perfect their art? Were there any dark secrets in their past?

Only they would know. Further along another poet Robert Frost caught his eye. James Trethowan had become obsessed with one of his poems. Often when working alone, he found himself repeating the same lines of one of his poems.

'The woods are lovely dark and deep and I have promises to keep and miles to go before I sleep'

Leaving the poetry section, he walked slowly along between the silent aisles of the A-Z authors. He studied the titles of many old masters. Beside them were new authors and their books with strange titles. Quickening his step past the huge volume of writers, James Trethowan stopped at the letter T. Selecting a few books by the same author 'Trevalyan' he returned to his seat.

He singled out one in particular entitled 'The Perfect Crime'. Opening it up he could see it had been loaned out often. The dates for receipt and return had a new page inserted. Why had so many people taken this book out? What was so interesting about committing the perfect crime? To kill someone was a violation of human life. Shortly afterwards he left the library.

Back in his hotel the receptionist gave him the keys of the cottage. A Miss Howard had left them with a message to call her when he came in. He rang her from his room. She informed him his bid had been successful and would call the next morning with some papers to sign. He thanked her, sat down and wrote a letter to his publisher in Paris and one to Miss Clarrisa Howard.

The next morning James Trethowan packed his small briefcase, posted his letter and left his hotel. He was dropped off by taxi at the bottom of the tree-lined avenue. Passing the huge white houses, he paused to gaze at one in particular. This was the house where he was born. The place where his parents had died in a mysterious accident. The walls were covered with thick green ivy. Dark shadows hung over the house as they had over him many years ago. Soon he was turning the key in the lock of the cottage which once belonged to his wife. Sitting down at the table, he took the original copy of 'The Perfect Crime' by Trevalyan from his briefcase, leaving the finished manuscript 'Nothing is Perfect' and the letter for Miss Howard beside it.

Rising from his chair, he walked slowly round the inside of the house. Out in the back garden he remembered his wife sitting completely absorbed in her work. How had she managed to work at her painting? Had the drive for perfection compensated for her dreadful hereditary disease? Later he locked the door and left the cottage.

At the end of the road he scrambled over the fence and headed towards the lake. Strong gusts of wind made walking strenuous. He and his wife had enjoyed this walk many times until it had become unbearable for both of them. After a struggle he was standing on top of the cliffside gazing down at the jagged rocks below. As if it was only yesterday he could see the twisted crumpled body of his young wife lying there.

Back in town Miss Howard had called at the hotel twice to no avail. She decided to go up to the cottage. Knocking at the door a few times without reply, she let herself in with the other set of keys. The young estate agent was puzzled, there was no sign of her client. Everything was as it had been the previous day, except for a book, a letter and a bundle of papers lying on the table.

Nervously she opened the letter addressed to her. A cheque for £200,000 was inside signed by James Trethowan. Picking up the book she looked at the title, 'The Perfect Crime' by Trevalyan.

Turning her attention to the bundle of papers, she looked at the piece of paper pinned to the front. Written in bold black ink was the title 'Nothing is Perfect'.

Later that day the body of James Trethowan was found lying at the bottom of the cliff.

Solace in Colour

Red silky petals
flutter in the wind.
Bright yellow marigolds
dancing in the sun.
Pale pink poppies
sway in the breeze.
Elegant lilac lupins
gazing at the sky.
White apple blossom
cluster on the bough.

A peaceful place
solitary thoughts.

The Collector's Thoughts

Fine sculptured lids never open or close,
eyes focused always in a sleepy repose.
The feathers arranged in perfect design,
claws sunk deep in the bough of the vine.

Pleasant and serene, this pride and joy
made by a craftsman who learned as a boy.
Patience and skill acquired over the years
passed on to the young, not without tears.

Learning this craft is a time to treasure,
a joy to behold where work is a pleasure.
Every featured detail is sharp and clean,
honed to perfection, by hand not machine.

Gazing in awe at this great work of art,
true love of nature has played its part.
Such creative designs of skill and flair
are infinitely timeless for all to share.

The Vacant Seat

Gaston gazed out of the huge bay window of his house. His eyes were focused on the seat in the courtyard. It was late in the afternoon; he could see the tall spires of the 'Montmartre' building glistening in the sunlight through the trees. His gaze quickly returned to the vacant seat. This was the first time in six months the couple were not sitting there.

Back inside his house, Gaston went through to his kitchen and made a coffee. He sat down and started to sip it slowly. Seconds later he rose up and hurried through to the huge living room to see if they had turned up. The seat was empty. He stared at it for a while, his mind turning over reasons why they hadn't turned up. Maybe they've had an accident.

Gaston Durieff had been forced to retire early two years ago from the post of Commissioner in the French Government. His power had extended to all the museums, art galleries and universities. With a special interest in the visual arts, the 'Montmartre' was a place he had spent much of his time. Unfortunately his wife had died after a mysterious accident, since then he had become a recluse.

Gazing out from the large bay window again at the vacant seat, he decided he had to go out. Gaston walked slowly up the road towards the 'Montmartre'. He gazed at the street artists working at their craft, but his mind was elsewhere. Why had the man and woman not turned up to sit as usual with their backs to France's most famous treasure?

When he arrived at the entrance, he immediately made his way towards the Gallery he had specifically commissioned for the Art of Photography.

Walking along he studied the pictures on the wall. He liked the black and white picture postcard size. Suddenly he stopped and gazed at one in front of him. Astounded he stared at it again, it was a photograph of the vacant seat in his courtyard. This time the seat was occupied by himself sitting reading his morning paper. Gaston Durieff realised the picture had been taken from inside his house. The window sill and the bay window were part of the print. He had an urge to tear it off the wall and look at the back of it. Gaston left the building and hurried back to his house. Everything was as he had left it. He studied the inside of the bay window and the floor hunting for any clues.

The situation was a complete mystery to him. The only time he had sat on the seat was with his wife to have his picture taken.

The next morning he rose early. Sitting at the bay window all day, he stared at the vacant seat almost willing the couple to appear. That night Gaston Durieff sat down and studied some of the old photographs of himself and his wife. He spent a long time looking at one he had specifically taken by a young man he knew who worked as a freelance photographer. He had met him previously in the 'Montmartre Picture Gallery' where he had struck up a friendship with him. Gaston remembered how meticulous the young man had been taking their picture. His wife had commented on how he had positioned himself in such a way as to always include the 'Montmartre' in the background. She never ever saw him again.

Gaston's mind returned to the picture in the 'Montmartre Gallery'. Had the young freelance photographer placed it there? This did not explain the absence of his wife in the photograph. The next day Gaston returned to the picture gallery in the 'Montmartre'. He went straight to the place to study the picture he had seen the day before. There was no sign of it. Not even a space where it had been. He searched high and low along all the rows of pictures, it had vanished like the couple on the seat outside his house.

Someone must have changed the layout. That was it. The picture has been moved. An attendant was standing close by watching Gaston, he approached him cautiously.

"Excuse me monsieur, can I help you?"

"Have the order of photographs on this wall been changed?"

"No, there are many famous pictures in here, we don't tend to change the position of these works of art."

"Why is it I can't find the one I was admiring yesterday?"

"Can you tell me monsieur, what is the content and name of this picture?"

"It is a seat with me sitting on it." The attendant looked at Gaston Durieff and decided to pass this enquiry on to his superior. He didn't like the way this man seemed so obsessed and was becoming quite irate.

"What is your name monsieur?"

"It is Gaston Durieff."

"I will inform the curator Monsieur Marat, he will be able to help you." The attendant left in a hurry to inform the curator.

"Gaston Durieff you say is enquiring about a picture?"

"You know him Monsieur Marat?"

"This man is well known to us at the 'Montmartre'."

The attendant accompanied the curator along to the place where Gaston had enquired about the photograph. There was no sign of the former commissioner. The attendant pointed out the exact place where he had said he had seen the picture the previous day.

"Did he say anything to you about the photograph?"

"He said it was a picture of himself sitting on a seat."

"Have you ever seen this picture anywhere in the Gallery?"

"No, I have worked here in this part of the Gallery for the past year, I would have remembered that face, it was something I'd rather forget."

"If he returns let me know at once, but not a word to anyone."

He hurried back to his office. Marat thought what sinister action he was planning this time. He remembered the death of Durieff's wife and the scandal of the missing photographs. Then there was the fire in the basement of the building. Durieff had been seen in the basement at the time. The curator was sure he had started the fire to get rid of some pictures he had stolen. The only witness who had seen him was his son Pierre the young freelance photographer. Shortly afterwards he disappeared without trace. A nationwide appeal and search revealed nothing.

Meanwhile Gaston Durieff had returned to his house. He hurried through to his small darkroom at the back of the building. It was here he developed his photographs. The walls were a smooth dark colour with pictures of shadowy human figures sitting on the seat in his courtyard. The room was menacing and threatening. Pictures and drawings of human torsos were stuck on one wall. Two big black metal barrels sat at one end of the room.

At the other end was a door with metal hangers welded onto the rusting steel. Stained waterproof capes hung limp and lifeless from the hooks. An old dark stained wooden cupboard come wardrobe was fixed onto the end of the metal sink which was very deep and more like a bath. The wooden cupboard looked strangely out of place in the metallized room.

Gaston opened the wooden cabinet and lifted out his old tripod and camera equipment. He carried it through and placed it inside the bay window, focusing it on the vacant seat. He sat waiting and watching. Occasionally he would glance up at the white spires of the 'Montmartre' piercing the white clouds in the distance. Two or three times he visited his darkroom. He checked the tripod and positioned it again. Gaston Durieff then took three photographs of the vacant seat. He carried his equipment back through to his darkroom. When he came back through the seat was still empty. He sat gazing at it for hours before going to bed.

The following day Gaston Durieff disappeared into his darkroom to develop the negatives of the photographs he had taken the day before. He emptied one of the steel barrels into the sink. Leaning over he stared at the pictures floating in the highly inflammable celluloid liquid. Reaching over he screamed in pain as the acid burned through his glove and into his hand. In the picture of the empty seat sat his wife and the young freelance photographer Pierre Marat. Guston Durieff gasped and fell forward into the caustic liquid, the photographs surfaced beside his body. He had died of shock resulting in a massive heart attack.

This is a collection of writing by,

Hans Callison

Published by Portbank Printworks 2009

What Am I?

I assisted in designing the Forth Bridges, but I am not an architect.

I helped build Balmoral Castle, but I am not a builder.

I help feed the starving, but I am not a caterer.

I help to heal people, but I am not a doctor.

I helped build a steam engine, but I am not an engineer.

I help feed the cattle, but I am not a farmer.

I help grow the flowers, but I am not a gardener.

I allow ships to dock, but I am not a harbour.

I am called upon to make gold rings, but I am not an ingot.

I help horses to ride on the field, but I am not a jockey.

I assist in ruling the country, but I am not a king.

I assist in repairing cars, but I am not a mechanic.

I help in looking after the sick, but I am not a nurse.

I aid people with their sight, but I am not an optician.

I assist government with pensions, but I am not a politician.

I help to prevent diseases, but not with quarantine.

I assist in a marriage, but I am not a registrar.

I aid in the making of a dress, but I am not a seamstress.

I assist in education, but I am not a teacher.

I am always involved in sport, but I am not an umpire.

I am the servant of a rich man, but I am not a valet.

I may be cheap, but I am not worthless.

I am always naked, but never X-rated.

I may be small, but not always a youngster.

If you don't possess me you will have zero.

What am I?

A coin that purchases the tools, the materials or the ingredients.

Look after me and I will always assist you.

The Wild Flowers of Tomintoul

In the seventies the blue tent was pitched
Sited behind the local school near the ditch
Their late twenties the occupants had reached.
Awakened by the cockerel call, their sleep was breached.
Eggs for breakfast was their treat
Tourist information was their beat
For the local activities to frequent
Coffee in the little café, their agenda of daily plans to make.
A trek through the wild glen, they ventured with guidebook in hand
A wild yellow flower dripping with dew
Never seen with the eyes of the Four
Snatched from the ground for closer view.
A second was plucked for its beauty of blue
A different colour was added to make it three
The birds in the brochure were nowhere near.
The red squirrel, the otter, the badger,
The pine marten and the deer seemed extinct.
Only the cows in the field created a stink.
The stunning views of the valleys appeared through the glen
Breathless they did stare, as the flowers became twenty.
The fresh air filled their lungs with plenty.
As they reached midway of the green arrow path
The flowers doubled into a posy of beauty.
As they reached the end of the trek
The last page of the descriptive brochure had been reached.
The voice rang out the last sentence to state,
Please do not pick the wild flowers.

The Squatters' Flitting

I had never seen my father and mother so excited, as they packed up to leave our squatters' house (something I didn't know until I was about forty years old) and head for our new house. They had received the keys the week before my seventh birthday on the 27th of February nineteen fifty-one. It was not a case of "do you want it or not"? You were glad to get a house anywhere. We were told we had to move on the 1st March to a brand new house in Gartlea about three miles from where we stayed in a room and kitchen at 201 Forrest Street, Airdrie.

Plans were soon put into action as tea-chest boxes were arriving into the house and being packed with our belongings.

On Friday morning, the 1st of March, a big van arrived and all the boxes and furniture were loaded onto the van.

Shanks, the farmer, arrived with his horse and cart and my father, uncle Pat and neighbours started loading all the stuff out of the big hut, out of the wash house and out of the coal cellar and onto the cart.

When the van was loaded my mother and three young sisters went into the cabin and went with the van. My two older brothers had filled the two-wheeled box barrow with coal.

The neighbours were left the rest of the coal. I went along with my brothers who were wheeling the barrow to our new house that none of us had seen. Everything was okay until we came to the hill, at which we had to push the barrow up.

Uncle Pat had gone with the cart and my father had taken his motorbike.

By the time we got to the junction of Broomfield Street, Hogg Street and Gartlea Road we couldn't push the barrow any more.

My oldest brother knew where the new house was, so he left us to watch the barrow, while he went to get my father.

We waited for what seemed like hours. My father came without my brother and without any problem wheeled the barrow up the hill, then down the steep hill to the new house.

It was my first view of the brand-new house. Planks were down on the ground to walk to the door. The rain had started. The smell of new paint greeted us as we reached the door. The warmth almost blew us back out of the house.

"Get your shoes off," rang out mum's voice "and leave them on the step." I could barely reach the handle to close the door

The living room looked dead big. I could just see out the windows, no curtains or blinds. What looked like a big beam ran right across the ceiling and a light hung from the ceiling.

I could barely reach the light switch on tip toes. "What are they?" I pointed to the plugs low down on the walls.

"They are electric plugs," all the older ones laughed. I ran into the kitchenette, which we called the scullery. There was a gas cooker, with oven, four rings and a hidden toaster. As well as a metal boiler, with a water tap to pour water straight into the boiler, and a tap to drain it. Two sinks, a shallow one and a deep one, with cold and hot water taps for both. A gas meter, that you put money into to get gas. A cupboard, with two doors at the top, one shelf in one and two in the other. Four drawers, at the bottom left, and a door to the right with no shelves.

A door led into the back lobby. Two shallow presses and an inside coal cellar. The floor was concrete and cold on the feet.

I headed upstairs. "The big room was mum and dads," said big sister. "That's our room," said big sister "and that's your room," said big sister "and that's the bathroom and the toilet."

"Dinner's ready, come and get it," shouted mum.

The Fungi Story

"Look!" She exclaimed like a child
"It's beautiful!" she squealed with glee
Pointing to the mushroom growing wild
Among the green velvet shaded by the tree.

Get the camera its beauty we must catch
As we gazed at the little wonder
Not another sight could match
With a click its beauty was captured.

Its face was crimson red
Adorned with speckles of white
Seated on its green velvet bed
We stared amid the streaks of light.

Witnesses to the wisdom of God's beauty
The brightness hidden in its glory
The small, frail creature of beauty
Alone it told the fungi story.

A Civic Reception

The invitation was received
A civic reception to attend
Discovery awards to receive
For a community of creative learning

The transport was laid on
For Motherwell we had to go
Orange juice or champagne in hand
Drowned out the waterfall of voices

Twelve seated at 39 tables
We were the last
Two litres of water
One of white and one of red wine

Eight small bottles of beer on ice
No chance of getting drunk
Unless you had the expensive taste
Of the alcohol at the bar

The three course meal
Was nicely presented
Served by students making ends meet
A helping that would create many a divorce

Celebrating the learning awards were made
Organised like a conveyor belt system
From Airdrie, Bellshill, Coatbridge, Cumbernauld, Carfin,
Croy, Glenboig, Kilsyth, Motherwell, Shotts and Wishaw they came

A piece of paper behind a sheet of glass to receive

All because they discovered the hidden talents of learning

In the present for the future

All at the paupers' expense

The thoughts of a sceptic.

Blame, Blame, Blame

Blame, blame, blame.
Lies in the heart of all mankind
Adam was the introducer
Messing with God's law of wisdom
Eating the forbidden fruit.

Blame, blame, blame
Lives like leeches in the soul
Adhesive to the flaming tongue
Matured by Satan's hope of impunity
Earning only distrust, danger, division.

Blame, blame, blame
Learned in the ranks of media politics
All play the game from top to bottom
Masters of twisting the truth
Envy is the damage of love.

One dark, dreary, night in November, Bob lifted a brick in Bank Street, Airdrie.

Then hurled the heavy object with all his might through the plate glass window of Penman's shop.

He then, put his hands in his pockets and leaned against the traffic light pole, as though nothing had happened.

The police responded to the noisy alarm and blue flashing light. When arriving they found no one else around, only Bob standing against the pole, looking as though he hadn't a care in the world.

Larry, the big burly blonde policeman, approached Bob and asked if he saw who smashed the shop window.

"It was me," replied Bob.

"It was you!" exclaimed the astonished policeman. "But why?" he thundered.

Bob shrugged his shoulders and started to walk away.

"Oh no you don't, it's Anderson Street for you!" blasted big blondie. As he stretched out, gripping Bob by the arm, gently leading him into the police van.

Bob made no fuss or showed any emotion while being apprehended. He had a few pints but was not drunk.

When they arrived at the police station, the desk sergeant, who was known to Bob, was bewildered by Bob's behaviour.

Bob was held until he appeared at court on Monday morning; charged with breach of the peace and vandalism.

He pleaded guilty; was given three months' custodial sentence.

After his release he met the big policeman who asked him why he smashed the window.

"It was the gateway to free bed and breakfast during the winter months," replied Bob.

Lines

In perfect formation they stood
Thirty four straight and good
Each one the same distance apart
Ready in silence to play their part.

The sound of scratching they felt
The thoughts of the writer did melt
Into the spaces words did creep
And filled with humour the sheet.

Told with fluid of black and blue
The story of deception so true
In creative language of the boss
About the four wheels he lost.

A good deed he set out to do
Soon he spotted the boys in blue
Forgetting he was full of the booze
His licence he was about to lose.

To the barman, the bill he still did owe
Over a pint of regret, told his woe
To the barman who in deception did phone
To drive, the message of deception home.

The Four Seasons of Life

I watched the tree blowing from side to side by the autumn wind
Its golden leaves fluttered to the ground
There was no mercy from the gale
One way then the other sometimes fast, sometimes slow
Sometimes gentle, sometimes fierce
Stripped bare of its coat, that protected it from the summer sun
How will it feel in the cold winter I wondered?
Only its thin layer of bark to keep it warm
When winter is over and the spring comes
New buds will develop into shoots to hold the leaves and its fruit
Ready to blossom in the summer sun.

I thought; a person's life is like a tree, living in the storms of the world
Four seasons: spring, summer, autumn and winter.
Four seasons. Of a person's life. Planning, production, sharing and resting
Spring is time of new life, of reproduction, of forward planning,
Summer the time of blossom, to display, to enjoy, to ripen
Autumn the time of change, to shed, to share.
Winter the time to shelter, to shiver, to tremble, to rest.

We suffer for we try to do everything in one season.

This is a collection of writing by,

John Cosgrove

Published by Portbank Printworks 2009

What Will the Robin Do Then?

The wind howls down the chimney
And blows renewed life
Into the banked up fire.
We sit secure and snug in our kitchen
While the elements strain to find
A weakness in the farmhouse's defences.

The windows rattle, and rain
Zigzags down the window panes
Jess and Spot lie on either
Side of the warm hearth.
Dreaming canine dreams of buried
Bones and mountains of Winalot.

A loud peel of thunder rents the air
"God's moving his furniture," grandpa says
The dogs rise and nudge his
Callused hand for a reassuring pat.
I am afraid, not really
But I would not mind a reassuring pat.

A bright flash brings me to the window
By the light from the house
I can make out the old elm tree
Cleaved in twain, its skeletal branches
Like fingers, pointing, accusing as though
I somehow had a hand in its demise.

"Go and tell Grandma to make us a brew
she won't be asleep, not on a night like this."
We three sit and sip Grandma's black-tar tea
A blanket of wellbeing, slowly descends over me
From the mantle, the Westminster chimes cheerily
Rousing me from my reverie
And one more childhood memory.

Traveling the Road

The hag's head rears out of a simmering sea.
A dark necklace of rain clouds,
Obscures the topmost crags.
I turn my the back on Spanish point,
At once silver droplets dance around my feet.
A tinkling prelude to the deluge.
Elements rage, cap and waterproofs my only refuge
Twenty-two rainy miles to Lisdoonvarna.

Up on the side of the purple hill
A white cottage squats, amid the floribunda.
I stand and listen in the rain,
In hope she will return to her song.
I know not of what she sings,
But her sweet voice lingers with me
Even after the melody has gone
My spirits now soar, as if on melodic wings
It's a mere twelve miles to Lisdoonvarna.

Old Sol now reigns supreme
And shines down on Erica and Ling
While Plantagenet dares to show its face
On mossy crags that never bore a crop.
A kestrel making circles in the sun
Surveys scars, that show the quest for peat
Nature's fuel that fires the native hearth
In the distance I can see the church spire of Lisdoonvarna.

The ribbon road winds down and round,

The church and graveyard predominate the sky.

I find the yellow shutters that I seek

My quickening pace takes me past the cross

I enter, and anticipate the taste of heaven

Tonight in this place there will be rare craic,

Strong drink and laughter.

Old songs will be sung and much music

Rare memories, will live forever amongst the rafters

And tomorrow, tomorrow my fiddle and I will

Travel on from Lisdoonvarna.

The Gardener's Lament

This year
Wisteria lost
To early frost.
Anemones and Asters
Horticultural
Disaster
Forget-Me-Nots
Best forgot.
Root rot
Black spot
Spider mites
Midge bites
Baby's breath
Done to death,
Slaters, slugs
And assorted bugs
Cat's urine
No columbines
The prize begonias,
Each one gonia
My hollyhocks are
In terminal shock
Thrips and aphids
Leave me crabbit.

The wife says, "Concrete slabs are best, why not save yourself a lot of stress?"

Stopover

The clang of a distant trolley car woke Bridgit up. She drew the drapes; even through the tinted glass she could see that it was going to be another wonderfully bright sunshiny Californian day.

Returning to bed she lit her first of the day. She had come in last night on the "Red Eye" from Chicago. The plane was busy, but the good thing was that first class was less than half full, so there was not a lot for Simon and her to do. She now had a four-day stop over, before she flew out to Hawaii. Her sister Kathy had moved out here two years ago after her marriage broke up. Last night at the airport she had met Richard for the first time. He seemed a lot older than she had imagined. The Tirrpitz family business was antiques. Kathy had met Richard in Dublin, where he had been visiting one of the many antiques fairs that are held there. He was on his second wife at the time, and they got married when his divorce came through. Kathy worked in the accounts department of Macy's, and they had agreed to meet in the food court for lunch.

She lit up her second cigarette, and once more made a mental note to try and give up. Maybe she could try hypnotism this time.

She heard the ring tones of a cell phone in the next room. Richard was on the phone for some time, some time later there was a tap on the bedroom door. "Are you decent?" said Kathy.

She was already dressed for work, "Sorry kiddo, I will have to take a rain check on our lunch date. That phone call you probably heard was to say that Richard's uncle Bertie had died down in Ensenada, and I will have to work through my lunch and late tonight if I am to get time off for the funeral at the weekend. We are driving down, stopping off to pick up Richard's nephew and his wife, they live in Foster City, we will probably be back late Sunday or early Monday morning."

Bridgit thought she saw Kathy give a disapproving glance at the cigarette butts in the ash tray. She wondered what her reaction would be if she knew that her older sister had three packets of a certain white illegal substance tucked into the lining of her uniform jacket.

"Sorry about this, but at least you will have the run of the apartment for two days and you will have Jasper for company. We thought about taking him with us but Richard thought it would not be appropriate. You will remember to take him walkies at least twice a day. I will be late in tonight, so just do your own thing, I'm already behind schedule, must dash, see you."

Bridgit did not bother making any breakfast, she took a taxi to Union Square, then walked down to the trolley terminus and bought a three-day-all-inclusive travel ticket. She suddenly realised how hungry she was. Lori's diner was almost empty. The morning breakfast rush had tailed off. She ordered eggs Benedict and some waffles. The waitress brought her the morning paper while she waited for her breakfast. The banner headline read "Tear grips the city" Last night there had been a murder in an up-market condo off Sutter St. A burglar had broken in and raped a young coloured woman, then mutilated her, stabbing her seventeen times. The reporter made the point that there had been four burglar-rapes in the last five months, and that this could be the same man, and that murder was the natural progression in these cases. The detective in charge of the case denied any connection with the rapes, but warned women living on their own to make sure their homes were secure. Bridgit was not the nervous type, but would be on her own for two nights with only a flea bitten mutt for protection. She smiled to herself, maybe she will meet a dark handsome Californian who would offer her night-time protection from rapists and such. Nevertheless, her next stop was the drug store next door where she bought a Mace spray. Late that evening, Richard and the sisters McGonnigle went for a meal in the Chinese town. The meal was lovely. Bridgit had thought they would at least have gone on to a bar for a few drinks, but because they were leaving early the next morning, they all went straight home. When they reached home, Richard's key would not open the front door. Kathy tried hers and it didn't work either. It took twenty minutes for the locksmith to appear. When he did he had to force the lock. He tried to repair it, but could not. The story was that the locks were special ones from Sweden and it would take until tomorrow to get the new part. The house-burglar alarm still worked so they would be okay for one night.

Bridgit woke up with the front door slamming, the bedside clock said five-thirty. She had to wait in for the locksmith. When he appeared, she noticed how handsome he was. When he had finished, she made him a coffee. Even Jasper seemed to like him. Over coffee he told her a few places to try if she wanted to sample what nightlife S.F. had to offer.

After lunch Bridgit took a trolley car down to Fisherman's Wharf and did the Alcatraz tour. When she returned she was walking along to Pier 39 when she met Simon and his "friend" Neville. They had a coffee and she was invited to meet them that evening at the Saucy Sailor gay bar in the Old Town. She went home and had a long hot bath, and had a few large G and T's while she was getting ready. Then just before she left for the Saucy Sailor's she snorted her last packet of the white lightning. The effect on her was almost immediate. She was up for anything now. Bridgit had a marvellous time. She got danced all evening, between dances she smoked some weed and tried champagne cocktails for the first time. Near the end of the night Simon and Neville had a falling out, a lover's tiff. Later Neville asked if he could share a taxi with her. Bridgit was no naïve teenager, she knew the score. The taxi had hardly moved off before Neville tried to put his hand up her skirt. She quickly put him right on that score. Later on she let him fondle her breast as a consolation. Neville saw her to the door. She gave him the key and he opened the door for her. By now she was feeling very drunk, yet she still managed to remember the numbers that deactivated the house alarm. She gave Neville a passionate kiss, and then she closed the door on him. First she kicked off her shoes. Then threw her jacket halfway across the room, and stepped out of her dress. By the time she reached the bedroom she was completely naked. Walking over to the bed she threw herself face down on it, and was asleep almost before her face hit the pillow.

Some time during the night she woke up. She sensed someone was in the room. Scrabbling for her Mace spray on her bedside table she cried out "Who's there?" There was a pause, and then she felt her hand being licked. Realisation came to her in a flash "Good boy Jasper, you look after your Auntie Bridgit, and I will buy something nice tomorrow." She turned onto her back and was soon asleep.

The light coming in through the window woke her up. She lay for a moment or two and realised she was needing the toilet. Feeling light-headed she managed to negotiate her way to the bathroom. Switching on the light she sat down on the toilet. The toilet bowl faced the shower cabinet. Looking up, her mouth opened. But no sound came. There dangling from the bloodied showerhead was the mutilated body of Jasper. She felt sick, and rising from the toilet she turned to the wash-hand basin. In the mirror she saw her naked body. Someone had drawn five bloodied fingers down her body from her shoulder down over her breasts down to her navel. That was when she fainted.

The noise of a telephone ringing roused her from unconsciousness. She tried to rise but could not. Her left leg would not take her weight. The telephone had stopped ringing. It took her some time to get upright. She had to get help. The telephone began to ring again. She hopped across the foyer and lifted the receiver. This was her chance to tell someone what had happened to her. Before she could speak a voice on the other end of the line said, "Animals are not the only ones who can lick." He sniggered, then the line went dead.

A Conservative's Prayer

Lord we thank thee for the quango,
And thy boon of privatisation.
Thou who once laid the lefties low,
Help us save the nation.

Thy people hath grown effete
A granny-state degrades
He who does no work, does not eat
Unless in shares, he trades.

The meek shall inherit the earth
Mayhap when they are dead.
Morality is of little worth,
Give me filthy lucre instead.

Lord you healed the sick, and thus
Extended their useful days.
The N.H.S is safe with us
With more for them as pays.

Lord God of the Conservatives
We heap bounty before thy throne.
Look after our friends and relatives,
And to the rest throw a bone.

Dear God to thee we pray
Let enterprise be free.
Yours and ours is the only way,
So shall it ever be.
Amen.

Good Kitchen

When ah wis a laddie,
Ma favourite day wis a Wednesday
We had mince and tatties then,
Wi' doughboys, an' ah dooked my
Breed in the gravy.

Tuesday wis an easy-oasey day.
It could be oatmealed herrin',
Shakey tammy or mebees tripe an' ingins
But usually it wis cabbage an'
Black puddins, aywis the horseshoe kind.

When money goat tight we fell
Back on the auld standby, soup.
The funny thing about the soup
It aye tasted better
For a day in the pot.

Ah am in here noo cause am auld
And there's naebody tae look efter me.
Ah still think back tae when ah wis a lad, and
The great tightners ma mither served up.
Ah never had a salad, till ah came in here.

Aye, they are big on foreign muck in here,
Spaghetti, pizza and that nippy mince
They ca' it chilli con carne
That's yer International Cuisine?
Ah hud better grub in the army.

Jist wance, if ah could go doon the Gallygate

An hiv efternin on the batter.

An then go tae the wulk shoap

Fur ah feed o' clappy doos.

Noo that's whit ah wid ca' good kitchen.

Have You Cleaned Out Your Drawers Lately?

The sideboard was full
It took two hands to open it. The other night
I managed it, without going red in the face.

In the drawer, was all things and everything
That we keep "just in case".

I found receipts two years out of date
A Yale key that fits no lock.
Five superfluous passport photographs
A pen and pencil set from Auntie Maude
Assorted coins from our travels abroad.
A postcard of the Turin Shroud
Several packs of playing cards unopened
My memory recalls card games now never played
Like Chase the Ace, Stop the Bus and Scabby Maid
A hip flask with a dribble of whisky in it
A leather cufflinks box full of trinkets.
Knitting needles of different sizes
Raffle-ticket books, that won no prizes
A biscuit tin full of buttons all
The wrong colour size or shape,
A box of paper clips, some pins and a measuring tape.
Sunglasses, spectacles and sun tan oil, long ago
Christmas menus for a lunch at the Tudor
Black and white photographs of
My dad in his uniform looking so proud,
And me at Blackpool, a young face in the crowd.
Book marks, phrase books and a calculator
Letters and diaries only fit for the incinerator.

Jacobite

Why do the redcoats beat their drums?
As if to warn us, that they come
Look you! There is as many as two score
The same again, by the loch's shore.

How did they come to know we were here?
Much English silver changed hands I fear
For not all Highland men are for the prince,
Let us away, we are spied long since.

T'would be folly, to stand and fight
We are but four, against their might
They think to have us at bay.
Guile will be our saviour this day.

Take my bonnet lad, tis me they seek,
May the prince's cause, give wings to your feet.
Away brave gallant, by way of Cragganmore,
And draw them to where the Corbie's water roar.

Rain clouds glower on darkening skies
As like a twelve pointer, he crests the rise
English voices fade away to the west
Young McIain is our bravest and best.

We travel by night and watch by day,
To Meldrum House we make our way.
For dry clothes and a guide to the sea,
Where a ship is anchored off the quay.

Now, Scot fights Gael, for English gold
A nation of lackeys, bought and sold
Freedom drowned in Culloden's gore
Gaeldom in servile chains once more.

They raze the crofts, evict from lands,
Those who against them ne'er raised a hand.
To exile we are forced to flee,
And spend our lives in penury.

God willing, we shall return once more
And tell tall tales of what went before
How we gave German Geordie a fright.
A toast our prince, and his Jacobites.

.

No Mean City

I dinnae like Glesca.
The wife likes it well enough.
Her ma, she steys there,
By Goad, she's a rough bit o' stuff.

I dinnae like Glesca.
It's awright fur a wee visit
The posters say, it's miles better
But is it?

I dinnae like Glesca.
Tramps hover aboot like vultures.
An' they aw sell the "Big Issue"
So much fur the City o' Culture.

I dinnae like Glesca.
Yir either blue or yir green.
Which school did ye go tae?
Ur you fur the Pope or the Queen?

I dinnae like Glesca.
The parking there is a joke.
If ye leave yir car it gets liftit.
The traffic wid make ye boak.

The wife's given me an ultimatum,
She's fed up stayin' doon the coast.
She's movin' back in wi' her mither,
If ah want a kin hiv a divorce.

I still dinnae like Glesca.

Though it's gave me a new lease o' life

Thanks tae that "Dear Green Place"

At last I've got shot o' the wife.

Sore Hearts and Silver Darlings

They beached their boat on Mingulay's shore
The blacked trimmed jib, said one was no more.
His share was left by the old sea wall,
Twenty silver darlings in an old grey shawl.

Home to their cottage, by way of the track
Off with the grey, and on with the black.
No tears she, though her heart was sore.
A new widowed woman, with no man to grieve o'er.

Three days syne, she sat by the strand
Watching the surf for her Calum to land.
In the bothy t'was said she would be fine
A cold wife now, but still in her prime.

They came from the manse, and spoke of her girth.
She would stay with them, till after the birth.
Not a sinner has seen her since that day.
Was it their pity that drove her away?

Like as not went out of her mind,
Losing her man, and so near her time.
Did the sea take her too, like the love of her life?
Was it the thought of being another man's wife?

This is a collection of writing by,

Jim Graham

Published by Portbank Printworks 2009

A Broken Mirror

Slipped from my clutches.

Beyond my grasp.

Upon the unforgiving terracotta,

The mirror smashed.

Fractured into slivers,

Myriads of reflection.

A minefield of broken glass.

Explosive retrospection.

A Good Wee Runner

I bought a car today.
A good wee runner.
It broke down after seven miles.
A right scunner.

I tried cleaning out the ashtrays
And doing a rain dance around it.
The rear axle had broken.
I was really in the shit

I'll never buy a car again.
It'll only end in tears.
It's just my fault for being wet
Behind the bloody ears.

Confidence

Take pride in your appearance.
Eat healthily and keep fit.
Show will power and true grit.

Have confidence in your decisions.
Think positive, be deliberate,
Discerning but considerate.

It's time to move on.
Embark on something challenging,
Amazing and worth imagining.

If you're hurting,
Don't keep feeling unforgiven.
Life is for living.

Gone Fishing

Spinning for trout
The reservoir high
Sma' rain falling
The drag on the Mepp was heavy
A bar of silver rose out of the water
I had the fish
Furiously reeling in.

Above, Concorde flew over
Its fuselage clear
So surreal.

"Beach" landing the fish
Disengaging the merciless treble hook.

A beautifully marked rainbow trout
Crudely battered on the granite
Bloodied and gasping
Refusing to die
I shared its distress.

London

Drawn to the 'bright lights'
But all they had to offer,
Were cold city people,
Divided both sides of the water.

The money doesn't go far,
Everyone wants to take.
Living on a student grant
And any cash I could make.

Breaking up with Mary;
She quickly found another man.
I lost my mind
Trying to understand.

Prayers for a Friend

Drawing from my imagination.
Staying indoors on a sunny day
Always me who's last to call,
Haven't spoken to anyone today.

If a stranger heard my story
Would they turn away
Or try to understand?
Solitude is just my way.

Making words form a poem.
Too abstract to comprehend?
Everything in God's time
Including prayers for a friend.

The Beautiful Game

Saturday morning football
On Glasgow's red blaes pitches.
Changing in spartan dressing rooms.
Foxy's amusing sex-life revelations.
The trainer's team selection.
Ralgex massages pre-match tension.

Our keeper's on the short side.
The McGuinns always carrying injuries
Big Alan's skilful, but lazy
And me, thinking I was Baresi.
Caught trying to play offside
And failing to take our chances.

No sporting handshakes
Only vitriolic post-mortem.

This is a collection of writing by,

Joe Higgins

Published by Portbank Printworks 2009

It's funny how things work out.

Ma day had started out no too bad; Ah had money in ma pocket, time on ma hands, not a care in the world, plus Ah wis looking forward to hot and steamie sex with a bit of tottie Ah had met the night before, so all in all things were looking good.

But fuck's sake – things dinnae half turn shitty quite fast.

Ah had picked three dead certs (or so Ah had thought) and Ah had nearly made it to the betting shop, when fuck it, who should come skipping round the corner? None other than 'Blade' McGurk – a right nasty piece of work and no wan o' ma best pals and fuck it – was he no team handed. Don't get me wrang – if it was just him, Ah would have taken him in a square go nae bother, but whit's a man tae do? You've guessed it, Ah ran like fuck.

Ah'm no too bad a runner. Which is just as well, cause these cunts wid have done me right in, aw because McGurk's sister said Ah horsed her! - My fuckin' arse. She's got a face like a bulldog chewin a wasp. Pure scrap man's dog material. It's just 'cause Ah had knocked her back.

So the chase was well and truly on and the stakes were high. You see, Ah'm quite attached to ma own arse, (who isnae?) but fuck, Ah wisnae even 30 seconds into the chase when Ah wis nearly caught. Ah wis runnin full tilt when whoosh, a fuckin' half brick just missed me. This is no going too well, Ah thought tae masel. If Ah could just make it to the woods Ah'd at least have a chance - a slim one - but still a chance. Ah knew those woods better than the dickheads that were chasing me. It was like a second home tae me when I was a nipper, plus Ah reckoned they'd split up and that would give me a better chance.

So there Ah wis, at full tilt, going for it, giving it ma all. Fuck, ah thought ma lungs were going tae burst and the sweat wis blinding me, but by fuck, Ah wis going to make it. Ah had only another hundred yards to go and then Ah'd be home free.

Ah made it, but still they were coming. Ah had nae time to think. Ah'd have to go deeper and try to hole up somewhere to get my breath back, Ah thought. Then Ah remembered 'Old Faithful'. It wis a tree no other cunt could climb when we were kids bar me, but that was a while ago. Fuck, if a lifetime truth be known – if Ah could get tae it, Ah'd be safe. It wis darker and scarier in there than Ah remembered, so Ah'd be able to use that to my advantage because they boys wur no for gein' in. But Ah was right, they'd split up, tryin' tae trap me. They'd nae chance. Mates.

Ah'd made it tae ma tree. Fuck, if anything, it looked bigger than it was, but nae bother, Ah bear hugged ma way up it. That was how nobody else could climb it and thank fuck for that now.

Ah'll tell you, being up there brought back memories – good mostly. Ah had spent many a happy summer playing in this big old tree. Made a swing in it, God! Ah even slept in it for a night and there Ah was hiding for ma life in it. Thank God for it. Those cunts were still searching everywhere for me. Nae luck lads. Ha! Ha! Ha! You'd think they would have something better tae do with their time on a Saturday than searching for me in the woods. Fuck it, Ah could stay up there all day and night and no bother.

There's a few stories attached to this old tree. It's the oldest in the woods and a few 'down in the dumps' have hung themselves from the branches of Old Faithful. It never bothered me any. If it wisnae this tree it would have been some other tree. This had been and still was my tree, just like a friend, it's always been there. Ah've been on every branch, smelled its leaves, felt its snarly bark and after all these years when Ah needed it, it was there.

Well the boys finally gave up the ghost... Mugs! And so it wis time tae climb down from my old friend. It had been good sitting there, remembering old times.

Ah'll probably come back with my own kids when Ah have them and introduce them to a very old friend.

Have you ever wondered about the people you pass on the street or the ones on the bus or train? Or the stranger who asks for the time, or the salesman who calls at your door? Uninvited new clergyman, the new neighbours or people asking for directions and I'm not trying to scare anybody or anything, but in this day and age, God, these terrible times, they could be anybody capable of anything. Just reading the papers is enough to scare anybody.

Murderers and rapists, kidnappers, junkies, pure evil people out there, you can trust nobody can you? And I should know because in a very short space of time, I've sent sixty-seven souls over to the other side. I don't know how many good souls or how many bad souls; well to be certain it must be about fourteen bad for certain. The first for sure, he was my foster parent; pure evil man he was.

The reason I was asking about all the strangers was that you just never know, well you'd never know by looking at me. I can tell you I've stabbed, shot, castrated, burned, poisoned and even beaten people to death, all of these people were strangers but two of them. My first and last victims, and I'm pretty sure I'll never get caught.

You may ask yourself why? Well it's a hobby, just like any other hobby, only more thrilling and let's face it when you're a seventy-six year old spinster living by yourself miles from anywhere, there's not that many thrills to be had.

You'll have to excuse me – I'm just off to make my uninvited guest more tea. He's looking a little peaky, the ropes must me too tight, bye bye for now.

This is a collection of writing by,

Rab Higgins

Published by Portbank Printworks 2009

A Crack in the Floor

I feel the needle prick my skin,
close my eyes and shove it in,
press the plunger and shoot it up!

I've got things to forget,
and this is my way,
it got so bad, I even tried to pray!

But my friends have been there for me,
and it's not as bad as people say.
Sure enough, I've still got my house,
OK, sure, my last cheque did bounce!

And yeah, my TV's gone, but that's alright,
because I like to read late at night.
And maybe yeah, I smoke some crack,
and that is why my teeth are black!

Four weeks later, here I sit,
in some flea-infested bedsit.
And before I know it, I start to pray,
Oh my God – I don't want to live this way!

So here's the point I'm trying to make,
if you take drugs – what a mistake.
And I don't believe what friends might say,
It's a terrible price you have to pay!

A Twisted Tale

JIHAD! Whit in God's name is a Jihad???

Ah only came in fur a kebab and a pizza. The next thing Ah know, Ah'm flat on ma arse and gettin' dragged through the back of ma local kebab shop - tied tae a chair and gettin' screamed at by guys who huv been sellin' me kebabs and pizzas fur years!

They're no' happy soldiers - there's nae banter an' jokin' the night. The looks on their faces tell me tae keep ma mooth shut.

Thank God. At last, someone who will get this madness stopped. Big Stevie. He's known me fur years - he'll get this sorted out. An' sure enough, he's raging, he starts shoutin' and pointin'. Fair enough, Ah huvnae a clue whit he's sayin' but he's no' happy about somethin'.

Then it all goes quiet. Ah count five of them, includin' Stevie and they're all lookin' at me! Then Big Stevie takes aff the bandana he's got roon' his heid and walks up tae me. Looks right at me as if he's never seen me before in his life. Walks round the back of me and blindfolds me with the bandana.

"Come on, Stevie man," Ah screamed. "Whit's goin' on here?"

Ah hear footsteps walkin' towards me. Big Stevie says that things are beyond his control. Ah shout, "You sound like a politician! Gies a break. Ah've been comin' intae yer shop fur years. Ah even tarred the roof on the fuckin' thing! Dae ye furget that?"

Big Stevie sighs an' says he's sorry but there's nothin' he can do fur me. Then he walks away.

"Come on lads. A joke's a joke - but fuck the hilarity! The wife knows Ah'm here. Dae ye no' think this'll be the first place that she'll come lookin' fur me?"

Somebody else walks towards me, ties a gag roon' ma mouth and laughs. "Course they'll look fur ye but by the time that happens, trust me, you'll be long gone!" Then Ah feel a sharp pain as a needle is pushed intae ma arm.

That's it. Ah'm never drinkin' again. Ah swear on ma ma's life. That's whit Ah wis thinkin' as Ah sat up. Then it all came floodin' back. Ah don't know whit they put intae ma arm. Ah don't want tae know, but Ah felt as if Ah'd drunk enough drink tae knock out the French fleet on shore leave. As fur ma mooth! Well, it seemed as if Ah'd been chewin' a sumo wrestler's jockstrap - after the fight! Ah looked round tae git ma bearings; It really hit home that these guys were deadly serious. This wis no ordinary room Ah wis in. For one thing the walls were metal and the door reminded me of the doors in the Bar-L. And then, Ah realised Ah'm baw naked. The shites had taken ma claes. Ah. Gies a break, there's nae need tae dae that - so Ah starts bangin' on the door, but that's no use. Too sore! So Ah sit doon an' Ah'm giein' it laldy wi' the soles of ma feet. That lasts about a minute, until Ah hear footsteps. They stop outside ma door an' someone barks at me tae get back fae the door. I shift back a bit an' the door opens. Standin' there is a guy who looks like they pictures you see in the papers. Ye know, guys dressed up in army fatigues. All Ah could see wis his eyes, cause he hud somethin' wrapped roon' his heid an' mooth. He flings me a pair of dungarees, ye know, like they things decorators wear. "Where's ma claes?" Ah ask him.

"Hud tae be burnt. The smell after your little accident meant that, shall we say, they hud tae be burnt. An' by the way, don't believe it if people tell ye it disnae burn. It dis!" An' with that he turns an' walks out an' bangs the door.

Ah'm pacin' the floor in ma cell when it hits me. They drugged me! Then they moved me somewhere, so it must be Sunday night! Aw naw! Ah run tae the door an' start bangin' and kickin' it. Ah must've been doin' that fur about 5 minutes, 'til Ah hear somebody comin'. Same routine. "Move back fae the door," the voice growls. Then the door is opened. "What do you want?" he asks.

"Whit wis the score in the Old Firm game?" Ah ask.

He looks at me as if Ah'm mad! "You have no idea how much shite you're in do you?" "Never mind the threats, just tell me the score will you?" He points his index finger at the side of his heid and starts turnin' it roon' - ye know, makin' the sign that Ah'm nuts! Then he slams the door shut.

Ah've no idea how long Ah wis in that cell, but it wis drivin' me mental. Ah fell asleep a couple of times. They brought me food. Ah don't know if they wir takin' the piss or not - but it wis always PIZZA they brought! Ah must have fell asleep again. When Ah woke up, they were four of them in the cell beside me, all dressed the same; army fatigues and their eyes covered. One of them was leaning on a chair. "Take a seat," he tells me.

"No' tae ye tell me the score in the Old Firm game," Ah says. They all started screamin' in their language. Ah don't know who pushed me, but Ah wis sent flyin' against the back wall. "Sit in the chair," Ah wis telt again. Ah got up and sat in the chair. One of them handed me a card with words written on it. Ah looked up and they had all moved in front of me, one of them holding a camera.

"When we tell you to read the words you will please do so."

I started, "We are very sorry for any inconvenience we have caused you but this will beat all your efforts YA TUBE. As Ah'm readin' this, all Ah can hear is sniggerin' an' gigglin'. Ah looks up and couldnae believe it. Standin' there is ma da, ma brother, ma wife and ma maw. Ah looked back down at the card. It said, "PTO," so I did. It read "Celtic 3 Rangers 0. Catch yersel on www.youtube.com HAPPY BIRTHDAY!"

How can playing fruit machines get you in so much trouble? For God's sake, I'm an intelligent guy yet here I sit in a stolen motor behind a bookies with a stupid mask over my face! I'll tell you, our Joe has a lot to answer for. Two grand he said for a day's work; don't make me laugh. If I get caught I'll be doing about ten years' porridge-that's if I get caught by the law. The clowns had only decided to rob one of Mick Fraser's bookies. Now that man has serious anger problems, just looking at him the wrong way wins you a trip to the casualty wing in the Monklands.

Well, as my old ma would say, I have made my bed so I'll have to lie in it. My God these masks don't half make you sweat. I'm sweating like a vicar in a brothel! How much longer are they going to be for God's sake?

Just at that, who do I see when I look in the wing mirror? Freddie Kruger, Frankenstein and the nut out of all those Scream movies all rolled into one. Just as well I've parked round the back of the bookies or if we get caught it could be a murder charge.

All it would take would be for some old dear shuffling along to see this drama unfolding, and she'd drop like a sack of tatties, suffering a massive heart attack.

"Drive! Drive!" That'll be Martin screaming in my ear. He was always over-dramatic, must think we're in an episode of the Bill. Now, in my smart way of thinking, I thought it would be better to just drive out nice and easy. No shooting out from behind the bookies like some missile. "Drive ya half-wit or you'll get us killed. Tell him Joe..." Now that would be Kano shouting, another one, this acting over-dramatic is contagious I thought -'til our Joe leaned over and said Big Mick was in the bookies. "So if I was you, ya knobhead, I'd get your foot down and head for the hills before the natives start to get their shit together!

So being in agreement with my new best buddies I slammed my right foot and floored it and that's when something strange happened. Another robber appeared right in front of the car. Well it looked like someone wearing a false face. For a second I almost stopped, 'til our Joe said, "Shite! It's Big Mick." And before you know it he's flying through the air like a goalkeeper on speed. I must have driven the car on autopilot for about a minute, 'til someone said, "You just killed Big Mick Fraser." I don't know who said it, but then I heard our Joe saying, "No. WE just killed Big Mick. That's if he's dead, because we're all in this together." By the time I had got my head round it all, I realised we were almost in Plains.

I nearly missed the cut off into the quarry, where our second car was hidden. I pulled up beside the Astra and we all jumped out. Kano went round to the boot and took out the fuel can and then splashed petrol outside and inside the first vehicle. We moved the Astra down to the opening of the quarry and waited for Kano to torch the car. We were taking a chance, torching the car this soon-but I had made up my mind earlier; head for Greengairs. Kano jumped into the car, fixed me with one of his manic stares and said, "It could have been worse. Big Mick could have caught us by now. Believe me, getting run over would be the least of our worries."

"No' kidding there," chimed our Joe. "I heard he raped some guy's wife 'cause he owed him fifty quid and was a day late with the payment. Ach, fuck him anyway. Good riddance to bad rubbish."

I don't know if they were saying all this to make me feel better but if they were, it was not having the intended effect. In fact, it was making me feel worse, because it suddenly dawned on me how mad these three were! As we were driving through Greengairs, Kano asked me to turn the radio on. I thought he meant for any news reports but he told me to put it onto Virgin radio as they play all the old songs from the eighties and even punk songs. I could hardly believe what I was hearing. Then to make matters worse, Martin pipes up and tells Kano to shut up as everybody knew punk was crap and the best music from that era was mod stuff like the Jam. " Ha!" Kano laughed, "The Jam were punks to start with." Straight up you would have thought we were all out on a family picnic.

"Shut up," I shouted caving in to the pressure.

Everybody went quiet before our Joe said something I couldn't believe, "There's no use crying over spilt milk."

I roared, "For God's sake, for all I know I could have killed Mick Fraser." The words 'could have' is the important thing here, after a couple of seconds,

I said, "Know something? Big Mick could be sitting in the back of the bookies, rubbing his hands, just thinking how much fun he is going to have with us if his mob can run us to ground. So forget that big dob of shite and worry about getting us safe, eh."

"They could have killed you Mick," said one of Fraser's two slacked-jawed stooges. "You're one lucky man. Are you sure you don't want to go to casualty and get looked at?"

"Sod that. I've got things to get on with. No one robs me and gets to spend the money. I want their names by 12 o'clock the night. I don't care what yous two have to do, or who you have to pay. Put it about that there's two grand for anybody who can give me the names of any of the clowns that were stupid enough to do this. Oh and by the way Seamus, and you too Pat - make sure you get the message across just how serious I am about this. On yous go and on your way out send Julie in will you?" Sweet perfume swirled around the back room. "Hello Mr. Fraser, Seamus said you wanted to see me." "Aye hen, come on in sit down. Pat tells me you phoned the law."

"I thought that was the right thing to do Mr. Fraser."

"How long have you been working for me Julie? Don't answer that. I'll tell you, you've been here ten year. And all of a sudden you start to think, ya stupid cow! Now, here's what you're going to do when the law turns up. For a start, you'd better stop that crying... right where was I? Aye, when the law shows up you act all innocent and tell them it's been a big mistake. Some of your boss's employees were only having a joke. No doubt they'll read you the Riot Act, but that's better than them looking into my affairs." Big Mick's bushy eyebrows creased, frowning over his angry eyes. "And they're going to have a good laugh at the very thought of some monkey turning over Mick Fraser. They'd love it." Fraser's brows lifted. "So be a good girl and get your mistake taken care of, will you do that for me, Julie?" There was a moment's silence. "There's a good girl. Now get on your way hen, I've got calls to make."

Big Mick started drumming his fingers on the desk, thinking to himself that it must have been an outside mob. "Nobody from Airdrie would dare rob me," he thought. Who would want to muscle into his manor and take their chances in an all-out war? His anger growing by the second, he was convinced no one would want that kind of trouble. If it had been locals, who would have been MAD enough to pull a stroke like that? There were plenty who would love to do it, but who was DAFT enough, because they would have had to have a screw loose.

Anybody hear the rattle?

Mixed Pakora

I knew where I was even before I opened my eyes. It's that smell, there's nothing on this earth that smells like the cells. It's a mixture of sweat, vomit and blood. It was a smell I was more than accustomed to.

The noise starts up as usual. It starts with one voice, then everyone joins in, and it's always the same "Whit time are yous gonnae let me oot?"

They always get the same response "Silence."

One thing about the Airdrie Police they are never in a great hurry to let you out in a Saturday morning. To be fair to them, they know that it is likely, more than half of those released in the morning will be back inside that night.

Something was different. They opened the cell next to me, passed me by, and opened all the rest of the cells. I jumped up and started bawling. What was the score I wanted to know?

The custody sergeant looked in the Judas hole. "When am I getting out?" I asked.

He told me to stand back, "You're not getting out just yet, CID want to have a word with you first."

"Whit dae ye mean CID wants a word wi' me there must be some kind of mix up."

"Nae mix up son, Kevin Beamish cell two, hold for CID questioning. That was what I was told when I came on this morning. Just cool it, one way or another it will be all sorted out in a couple of hours."

"Cool it, you must be joking." That's when all the wee motors started driving around my head, and began bumping into each other.

I sat back down on my mattress, and thought what in God's name would the CID want with me? I had done nothing. OK I was drunk and maybe a bit too loud, but nothing for them to get involved with.

How fucking wrong can you be?

I must have dozed off, because the next thing I know I am getting tapped on the head by someone's shoe.

"Let's be having you Kevin, are you sobered up yet?" a voice said.

I looked up, these two did not look like CID to me. They were dressed in casual clothes, jeans and T-shirts. Both had casual jackets on, one leather the other a Wrangler jacket.

The one in the Wrangler jacket helped me up.

"Let's go mate, this should not take too long."

I stopped outside to put my shoes on. "You won't be needing them just yet," I was told, as they walked me down to the outer door.

We waited until the duty sergeant came to open the door for us. I said to him "What's this all about?" Not a word did he say, but he gave me a pitying look.

I was led down one corridor after another finally we stopped at a door marked 'Interview Room'. I was ushered in.

"Sit down Mr Beamish."

"Listen I…" he stopped me.

And I was shocked when he said "We are not police officers we're from MI5."

I started to laugh so hard I almost pissed my pants. I could not see the two jokers for the tears running down my face.

"MI5, aye that will be right, I don't know who put yous up to this but I'm not falling for it."

Suddenly it did not seem so funny when the guy with the Wrangler jacket said, "Mr Beamish the evidence we have against you at this time could put you away for thirty years. So if I were you I would start taking things seriously, very seriously."

"I'm not having this," I said, "I want a fucking lawyer."

"You're not under arrest Mr Beamish," said leather jacket. "Under the new home security laws you can be held for questioning for up to twenty-eight days. We know who you are Kevin, is it alright to call you Kevin?"

Smiling he said, "My name is Smith and his is Jones. Now if you are a good boy we can do this here, or if you prefer we can take you to a secure unit, you're choice."

I said, "I don't know what you are fucking on about, but I've got nothing to hide." At that moment there was a knock at the door. Smith got up and answered the door, he came back to the table holding a folder.

"Right Kevin what is your association with Mr. Azul Gulzar?"

"Who? I don't know any Azul Gulzar."

He opened the folder and slid a photograph across to me.

"Do you know this man?"

"That's Terry from the kebab shop."

"I can assure you that this man is Azul Gulzar, and at this moment he is being held in London with three of his associates after trying to car-bomb a shopping mall in Islington."

"I still don't see what this has to do with me."

He opened the folder again and slid across four photographs of me carrying four Calor gas bottles into Terry's shop. "Mr Beamish the car bomb that Mr Gulzar and his friends were caught with contained three gas bottles that we can trace back to you. What with the nails and bolts. Have you any idea the damage to innocent shoppers, men, women and children this bomb could have done?"

I felt as if someone had just booted me in the balls.

"Alright Mr Smith and Jones or whoever you are, I think I am being railroaded here. Back it up a bit not so fucking fast. This guy you call Gulzar of course I know him I buy my kebabs from him. He asked me to do a repair on his roof. That's where the gas bottles come into it. I needed one bottle for the burner to boil the tar, and he asked if I could get him three small ones for the Calor fires in his house. It's as simple as that I can't see Terry being a terrorist. For fuck sake he runs a Kebab shop."

Smith slammed his hand on the table, and made a grab for me, but Jones held him back. Smith shouted at me, "Have you forgotten what these bastards tried to do at Glasgow Airport? Well what they were trying to do in London would have caused twenty times the damage. I am not convinced that that story of yours rings true. So stop playing silly buggers and go over your story again." I went over my story again.

There was a lull in the interrogation. Jones slid me over another photograph from his folder.

"Do you recognise him?" said Smith.

Now this guy I did know, and I told them. When I told Smith and Jones they got very excited.

"Are you one hundred percent sure you know him?"

"I am one hundred percent sure I know him," I said.

"Now you are not bullshitting us are you, you really know this man?" I nodded.

"Did you meet him at Mr. Gulzar's house?"

"No that is Sharif Khan, he has the off-licence two doors down from Terry's kebab shop. Well that's the name I know him as, no doubt you will tell me it's different."

"Kevin, the man you have just identified is one of the most wanted men in Britain, if not the whole of the western world."

"No shit! Now do you believe me? I'm no terrorist, and I'll tell you something else he wants me to tar his roof."

"When does he want you to do the job?"

"As soon as possible I suppose. I have his mobile number in my wallet."

Smith said, "We have to put you back in your cell. There are people we have to speak to on how we are to proceed."

I said, "Ok but could you give me a packet of fags and a lighter? I'm choking for a smoke."

Jones put his hand in his pocket and handed me a packet of Rothmans and a lighter. He said, "Knock yourself out Kevin, you deserve it."

They came back in about an hour. Smith threw me my wallet. "We have the green light to go ahead. You don't have a problem with that do you? If you do, say so Kevin. But if you help us you will be doing your country a great service."

"Fuck me, two hours ago I was a terrorist, now I'm the saviour of the western world."

"Unfortunately that is the world we live in Kevin. The guy standing next to you in the toilet could be a terrorist. Because you are white and Scottish does not mean you are not prepared to go to jail or kill for some cause or other."

"Here's the script," said Jones. "Tell Sharif you will do the job tomorrow, but need money to buy the materials."

"Hold on," I said "That won't work. He knows I'm a bevy merchant. He won't hand over money to me on Saturday. He knows I would blow it. It will have to be Sunday night."

"Whatever, all we want is him out in the open so we can take him down... You know now what this means, we will have to take you to a safe house for today and tomorrow. We will have someone with you all the time. Tell Sharif you will meet outside his shop on Sunday night."

I said, "Before I make this call, let me get this straight, when you have this madman dubbed up that's me done, nae courts or any o' that shite?"

Smith said, "I promise you Kevin, when we have our man, you are free to get on with your life. No courts no nothing."

I made the call. I will tell you I would have made some spy, either that or I'm just a good liar. Sharif agreed to meet me outside his shop after closing and give me fifty quid for materials. Smith and Jones were pleased.

I was taken to a hotel in Coatbridge. The time leading up to the operation was a nightmare. They went over the drill maybe a hundred times. I was to drive up to the shop and pump the horn and stay in the car and let Sharif come to me, easy peasy as they say.

I am sorry if you are disappointed, but that is exactly what happened. I drove to the shop pumped the horn. Sharif came out and walked towards me. He was jumped on by some men in black. The last I saw of him he was handcuffed and sitting in the back of a black Range Rover. Mr Smith drove me home, thanked me for my help then he drove off.

Now the funny thing is there was never any mention of a court case, and no mention of Sharif or Gulzar appeared in the papers. Gulzar's shop never opened again, and Sharif's is now owned by a Pole.

Needless to say I never heard from Smith and Jones again…

Reg

A funny old guy,
his stories you could not buy,
words of wisdom he gave for free,
and a true friend he was to me.

He took you as he found you,
and if you lied he always knew,
but judge he did not,
and his friendship could not be bought.

And now he's gone – but I won't shed a tear,
instead I'll hold all my memories dear,
of an old gent and a scholar too,
and a friend who was always true.

True Romance

Two words broke my heart
The words sounded like a scream
There's no-one else but, "We're finished!"
I want to make a fresh start

Have I done something wrong I pleaded?
No we've just grown apart
We can't leave it like this tell me
You have not given me what I've needed

What about the times we've shared
They will always remain special
To me they seem like a lie
Please believe me I always cared

When you walk out the door it's over
You'll meet someone new give it time
I feel like a leaf out of season
You were more than that you were my lover

I think the love came from one side
That's a lie I gave as much as I took
From what is being said you are the one takin'
Be a man stop trying to hide

If you're leaving just please go
But there's so much to be said
I believe we've said enough
But I don't want to leave when you're so low
Just leave and don't let the door hit
You on the arse on the way out doll.

This is a collection of writing by,

Iain Johnston

Published by Portbank Printworks 2009

The Witch Town

To Edgar Allan Poe

Still lies the old town, amid hollow and hill
Long gone are they that lived and thrived here
Idle are its forge, its church and its mill
Left only now
Are desolation and fear

By day as silent as some olden monarch's tomb
No bird song, rattle of wheel, or horse's neigh
Only crumbling gambrel roofs and rooms of shadowed gloom
Lonely graveyard, cracked stones
In loam and clay

For at night with dull toll of steepled bell
When strange moon shines over misty cloud
Rise shapes awakened by some necromancer's spell
Floating hither and yon
With wail and mouldering shroud.

At the sepulchral tolls within hoary steeple
Arise now fleshless forms on yellowed bones
Imbued with an infernal life are those knighted people
As an incantation from deathless lips
Mutters and drones.

Mindful are we of the old witches' tales
Of stern Puritan justice, of trial, rope and fire
Of dark rituals in hidden valleys and dales
Of half-glimpsed things
Nightmarish and dire.

On gallows hill many a witch and warlock hung
Through the tones of that ancient rusting bell
By ghostly hands at stroke of midnight rung
Calls them back from the bourns of hell.

The Pastel Rainbow to A Glasgow Street Artist

Kneeling on cold pavement, working away
A battered tin of Greyhound pastels all you had
In heat of summer, or dreich winters day
Discoursing on times when you were a lad
Of war and the hell of Suvla Bay.

I recall again a cheery, grizzled face
Faded medal ribbons worn with glowing pride
Eyes that stirred, still with a dreamer's gaze
On that bridge above the River Clyde
And the city's smoky tenement maze.

Forest glade, ocean tide, swans on a lake
Spectrum dusted fingers, creation with an angel's touch
Magical scenes, slumbering dreams that came awake
Rembrandt, Gauguin, all would have bowed to such
Art was there then, only for arts' sake.

I believed you were immortal, would never die
Then one spring day you were no longer there
You had passed on without regret, murmur or sigh
Hurrying feet smudged those dreams without thought or care
Was then I saw the pastel rainbow in the sky.

The Haunted Road

Walking to Loch Rannoch at Night.

Dark and forbidding was that country road
That wound through jagged hill and glen
Where warring clans of yore once rode abroad
Round lochan and bracken coated ben.

A haunted path o'er Killiecrankie's ford
Where redcoat and highlander still fight
Spectral rattle of musket and sword
Phantom forms furtive in that sable night.

Alone I walk with shadows of former years
Along that rough and trackless drovers' way
On and ever on towards the valley of tears
My travel lit by ghastly moonlight's lambent ray.

The black waters of Loch Tummel are awhirl
An eerie wind stirs the lofty swaying pine
Rises in pitch to a witch's skirl
Then sinks to a demon whispered whine.

From Schiehallion's lofty peak the wild eagle calls
Sunlight comes dispelling a night dark and drear
A gleam then o'er that fairy mountain's halls
Drives away those formless shades of fear.

Cois A Bhile

The Place of the Sacred Yew

A poem to the oldest tree in Scotland.

Stood I here for nine thousand years
Though my heart has died and my limbs grow weak
Trunk scarred by Druid's sickle and Neolithic spears
Outliving my kindred, oak, ash and teak
I was young after the glaciers melt
Saw new races pass below my shade
Pict, Milesian, Danaan and Celt
At my roots Saint Ninian knelt and prayed
'Neath my greenery the little people did peep
The woodland echoed to their fairy song
Ever gone now they into an eternal sleep
For the sound of Elvin pipes I listen and long
I have heard the rhythm of the Gaelic plough
Then a young man unto the Holy Land sailed
Once who played amongst my leafy bough
And the Son of God to a cross was nailed
With blare of trumpet the legions came
Helmets and standards shone in the sun
Only dimly do I remember Rome's fame
For still I exist and their story is done
Dwell I at the entrance to the Glen of Lugh
Above the blue waters of great Loch Tay
Beneath a majestic sky of azure hue
Where golden eagle and plumed hawk hold sway
Long may I stand, a venerable yew
Through solstice sun and winter storm that rages
Symbol of Caledonia, lionhearted and true
Stout guardian from the dawn of ages.

The time has come. We line up expectantly. The last drink of saki has been taken. The final words said. The General climbs back into his dun-coloured staff car.

Was that a tear upon his cheek? A tear for his boys, the protégés he would never see again?

Though, we are happy. We go as heroes. I glance across at Kobo, my old school friend, now a comrade-in-arms. I am jealous of him. He will fly one of the jets, the ones sent by Germany. Messerschmitt 262's, carried by submarine to our shores, sleek deadly machines.

The sun rises upon us for the last time: the sun is the symbol of our nation and of our God-Emperor. We wear the sign of the cherry blossom on our tunics and scarves. On our flying helmets are fixed mottos.

At a shouted order the bomber crews run to their machines. In the bomb bay of each of the camouflage painted Mitsubishis, lies a 'Baku' the small rocket driven plane with the explosive nose. Such a craft will I pilot against the ships of the 'Keto.'

Propellers start to spin, engines to roar. With a final 'Banzai!' we race in the wake of the bomber men. Eager hands help me aboard. The plane takes off, climbs high. Smiling eagerly, carrying my two-handed sword which will go with me, I make my way through the interior of the bomber. There it lies, my aircraft, swaying in its cradle.

It is a stubby, squat contrivance with a twin tail and small cockpit, painted sky blue and emblazoned with the scarlet circle of our sun. I raise the Perspex canopy and climb in, closing it for the last time. The controls are simple - a child could fly it. I settle in and wait.

The air fleet I am part of speeds towards the besieged island of Okinawa. This aerial armada, this winged nemesis, is composed of a myriad of machines. Zeroes, Vals, ancient Nakajima, flying boats and fighters. All on a one way trip.

The giant plane, my carrier, shudders suddenly. Anti-aircraft fire! We must be approaching the allied fleet and the embattled island. More shudders. A light glows on the instrument panel. I am about to be released. I think of my family and how they will light a candle for me at the shrine in my mountain village.

The Kamikaze; they have named us after the divine wind that once saved our sacred islands from the fleets of the Great Khan. Now our attack will scatter the ships of the Keto and our glorious history will repeat itself!

Then I feel the bomb bay doors swing open and my machine falls free. I glance up quickly. The mother craft has been struck. Her starboard engines are aflame. I ignite my motor. It coughs to life and I am slammed back in my seat. I ease the controls forward and down.

Below, like great whales, lie the vessels of the enemy. White water foams in their wake. Cruisers, destroyers, battleships, troop transporters, carriers - I have time to see them all.

I observe other rocket planes diving, their tail units plumes of flames. The Zeros are going in, wave after wave. Tracer erupts upward, a death dealing kaleidoscope of colour. Then a Zero falls trailing a stream of fire. It disintegrates. A shell bursts near me. The Perspex cracks. The enemy craft are nearer. Several are afire. I search quickly for a target. A few minutes more I will live as a mortal. It is strange to think I will never see sunset over Mount Fujiyama again. I smile as I think of the paradise awaiting.

Below, the ships are closer. I see the flash of gun muzzles. My plane shakes at near misses. My smile broadens even wider as I see my target, a small carrier already hit. It is burning in its mid-section.

I put my rocket plane up to top speed, knowing nothing can stop me. Faces glance up, mere indistinguishable blobs beneath steel helmets. They run about, away from my downward plunge, two legged ants in denim. Damage crews are trying to ditch their own burning planes over the side. In the great conflagration I see the twisted skeleton of a Messerschmitt. Is it Kobo's? He always beat me in everything in school.

The deck spins up. I aim for the undamaged bridge. I glimpse the startled countenances of the American Officers. Can they see me, their nemesis? Do they, in this split second of their terror, see my face? The yellow face, goggled, in fur-lined helmet. The face of the hailed Nipponese. They scatter frantically.

I cry one last 'Banzai' my free hand grips the hilt of my sword. Then I strike!

Home is the Sailor

(A Story of the Future)

The Starship "Charles Eric Maine" had returned from the stellar system of Rigel after an exploratory voyage of forty years earth time. It was the greatest event of the twenty-second century. Virtual reality viewers throughout the solar system, on the nine planets, fifty moons, a myriad of space stations and mining colonies in the asteroid belt saw their heroes come home. Men who still looked only five years older having travelled at near light speed.

Then after the ceremonies, the ticker tape parades, the medal pinning, the interviews, after all the pomp and media attention, then came the cold reality…

Captain Stuart Conroy picked the cab up at Aberdeen Stratoport. Forty years ago, when he had last hired a cab, it had the convenience of a human driver. It had been a jet copter. This one was automatic and anti-grav. The changes around him were beginning to sink in.

As the globular craft swung over the sky reaching the towers of Glasgow's east sector he leant back and gazed out. Many old landmarks were gone including the gothic spires of the University. The motorways in and out of the city, once the pride of the twentieth century were cracked, overgrown and neglected by a society that had conquered gravity.

He lit a cigar. An automatic voice filled the cab.

Please do not smoke in this convenience as it is bad for your health and has officially been banned from all air transport since twenty-one thirty by the world council.

The port on the starboard side of the craft hissed down.

"Please dispose of it now," continued the tinny voice.

In disgust Captain Conroy tossed the freshly lit cigar from the cab. He was nervous enough about going to see his son without something to soothe his nerves.

The grav-taxi dived suddenly down to the suburb of Knightswood. Once an ancient mining village now a conglomeration of automatic factories. The cab landed gently on the giant pad, a parking and maintenance facility for anti-gravity vehicles that had once been Knightswood Park. He descended to ground level by grav-tube.

The wide walkway was flanked on both sides by identical domed housing units. The humming sound of the autofacs came to his ears, distant and regular. It gave him a sense of pride to know that his son was the human manager for the whole region. His son would now be older than he was. A father thirty five and a son over sixty. Man had yet to conquer the time barrier. Perhaps in time a faster than light drive would be developed, but for now, Einstein's M.C. squared was still a very cold equation.

The thoroughfare was deserted at first. Then the group of youngsters spotted him. Spotted the tall broad shouldered man in visored cap and space- black uniform with coloured insignia. A man who walked with the catlike stroll of all spacemen.

Gosh! It's Captain Conroy! Hey! Captain, saw you on the tele-vid. What's it like out there? What about the Rigellians?

He paused in his stride, irritated by the attention of these bright-eyed boys, forced a smile, handed out a pile of signed holograms of the crew, the ship and himself; answered the same old questions. Then they were gone. The rapid patter of their receding feet and eager voices fading with distance.

"Wait till I tell dad I saw Captain Conroy." "Yeah! And we got signed holo-pics too."

"I'm going out to the stars myself when I'm old enough."

"Yeah! You do that," thought Conroy.

"Then you will be the loneliest man on the planet."

He thought of the immense blue sun, Rigel and its one inhabited planet, of the tall blue arachnid inhabitants and their great, world spanning webbed cities, a race that lived in close harmony with nature. A machine less society existing in symbiosis with all the life forms they shared their world with. A peaceful civilisation much of whose medical knowledge could cure all the epidemics and morbidities that tormented mankind, Aids, cancer etc.

The Rigellians had a lot to teach humanity. He knew one Kashallin had returned with them as an ambassador, eager to study the culture of the new strangers that had come from the stars.

He came to the domicile of his son. He felt awkward. He stood for a few moments; he had painful memories of Martha, gone twenty years. They had shared this home, had reared their son in it while he, Conroy, had been on the Earth-Mars run. Conroy, the space pilot, best in the fleet. Then had come the chance to command the Earth's first Starship.

It had been too good to turn down. Space was in his blood; always had since as a wide eyed child he had gazed with awe through the space port fence at the lunar ferries rocketing up. Conroy had been taken there by his father, a test pilot, a tall blonde man in R.A.F Space Command blue, who had died later testing out a new ion drive moonship leaving him fatherless.

Yet he understood and did not feel bitter. It was the urge passed down from father to son. He only hoped his own son would now understand.

With hesitant steps Conroy walked up the path. A red light blinked on the porch notifying the occupant that he had a visitor.

The curved door slid back and there stood his son, Sean. Forty years had made a difference. There were lines and wrinkles in the face. Once fair hair was now shaded grey. Had it not been for the scholarly stoop Conroy would hardly have recognised his son.

"Sean Boy!" He spoke awkwardly, his hand held out. There was silence for an electric period. The son did not take the proffered hand.

"I saw the return by Vi-video," Sean's voice was slow and steady, unwelcoming. No trace of warmth in it. "You'd better come in then," a reluctant phrase... Conroy entered his son's living quarters. Ushered into the main room the Captain's eyes moved swiftly around. Modest and comfortable. A tri-player, vi-video screen, automatic furniture. His gaze drifted towards the mantle. Pictures of Martha and his son. None of himself. He had a sinking feeling.

"Why did you come?" Sean asked coldly.

"To see you of course," stated Conroy.

"I would have thought this would have been the last place you would want to visit. After all we never had much in common," Sean's words were full of bitterness. "You were selfish dad. You chose space instead of family life. Oh! Yes, you left us well provided for but we were never a family after you left."

"I had to go Sean. You don't understand the urge. You never did. Man has to go out there. It's part of our destiny. New worlds await us."

"Yes, I know about your new found friends. Those big gentle spiders. That's all you found so far, isn't it? Good job really you came, I suppose. I'm dying of leukaemia. I've only got two years left."

"Sean!" Stuart Conroy's face twisted in pain. "I didn't know."

"Well you never did care, did you?" Sean almost shouted. Stuart Conroy almost grabbed his son by the shoulders then.

"That's it! Didn't you hear the broadcasts? The Rigellians are natural doctors. They can cure almost anything, including leukaemia. They can do it overnight. Cure millions. Don't you think those forty years on the Maine expedition were worth that? I cared enough for my fellow man to make that sacrifice, to return to a dead wife and a son older than I am."

Sean Conroy, still bitter, retorted "Don't give me any platitudes. You really wanted to go out there. Not for any altruistic motive. Did you really think I would accept a cure brought back by you?"

They must have talked thus for a further two hours, Conroy trying to reason with his son, now an old man and the son denying a father forty years younger than himself.

At the end they parted. The son escorted his father to the door.

"Oh, and Dad. Don't bother coming anymore," were Sean Conroy's parting words. The Captain never looked back. He had turned away from his past. Now only the future lay ahead. It was dark. Hosts of stars, silver-speckled dust in the infinite called him back to the only home he now knew, that of endless space.

Somewhere an orbital shuttle roared up on its retractable plasma jets.

He gazed up at it yearning. He had no regrets, men of his stamp never do. Ever since man first gazed skyward the urge had been there. The urge that had sent men seaward with full sails. The urge that made the early settlers and their prairie schooners start on to a virgin west. That had sent balloons and crude aeroplanes aloft. That had placed the first footprint on the moon.

He thought of the old poem. How did it go?

"Home is the hunter, home from the hill. The sailor home from the sea."

Though at times there is no returning, Conroy's eyes sparkled like the stars as he saw the great black void. The urge called him home. Above, the beckoning, eternal lights twinkled.

'Lartia' A Tomb in Tuscany

In the smoky dusk of twilight I did walk alone
Perchance, to come upon that ancient quiet place of rest
A crumbling silent sepulchre of age-worn stone
Above the entrance, a long, forgotten and faded noble's crest.

Memory stirred within me of life lived long since
When Etruria was great among the nations of the earth
Then I loved the maid, Lartia, and I a prince
And she the keeper of my wealth, household and hearth.

Yes! We lived and loved within those spacious marbled halls.
Till one eve I fell into a dreamless, timeless sleep
To awaken in a future age to Etruria's ruinous walls
Now for my long lost love I can only weep.

So, before this tomb where lies fair Lartia, my love
That peerless damsel of beauty and flowing raven hair
I beat the ground, curse gods below and above
Those heartless deities we worshipped that didn't really care.

My eyes are dimmed, awash with endless tears
The maiden, Lartia, to bone to dust has long gone
Her laughter is but an echo, now fading in my ears
My grief, within me, sings a sad eternal song.

The Blemish on the Buddha's Smile

I had stopped to rest that afternoon on my wearisome journey. The sun was hot, hot as it can be in the Orient. I had walked far that day on my aimless travels. Up winding mountain roads that had known the rampant tramp of armies and the solemn tread of pilgrims for untold centuries.

Below me, the panoramic view spread out, revealing to my gaze miniscule villages clinging to precipitous slopes, buildings and antique temples; showing that quaint style of architecture that appears to reflect the spirit of oriental mystique to occidental eyes.

A small white stone shrine attracted my attention, half concealed by leaning, wind swayed trees and flowering foliage. The building appeared extremely well kept even though it gave the impression, at the same time, of very great age. The stone used in its construction had obviously been quarried in the valleys below and then carried up the steep torturous paths by the devout, in some forgotten era of the far past. The shadowed entrance was guarded by two stone lions, mute sentinels, the "Chindits" that are found in front of such edifices.

Intrigued by its solemnity I entered into the coolness of the seemingly deserted fane. A faint aroma of incense lingered there. Light shafted through tiny windows alighting with a mellow glow on the immense statue of the Buddha that reared in grandeur at the very centre of that quiet temple.

I gasped in awe! Surely this great carving in marble was by the hand of some master craftsman? Certainly the work of a Michelangelo of the Asian peoples.

I stood, mesmerised by the beauty before that great work of art. I marvelled at the well chiselled graceful body. The benign expression on the countenance; the bowl in the lap enclosed by the well sculpted hands. I threw a few coins into the proffered receptacle as was the custom in this land that bordered on the limitless expanse of China.

The tinkling as they spun into the marble oval broke the stillness that had prevailed since I had entered silently. The sound of sandals on stone and a discreet cough made me turn.

He was tall for a representative of the saffron-skinned races. He wore the plain robe of Sangha, the order of the Buddhist Monks, a familiar sight in the far eastern states. His face was of an indeterminable age. Though the lines upon it gave the hint that here was an individual who had had it hard in life and experienced traumas far beyond that of the ordinary human ken. His smile and the gleam of eye were of that radiant quality that the truly spiritual have the world over. He addressed me in a voice that was of strong timbre and well-modulated.

"Greetings wayfarer, welcome to this most holy ground. I see you have been admiring the statue of our Lord Gautama?"

"Yes! It is indeed a marvellous work. The man who created it was indeed an artistic genius."

"That is indeed true," he replied.

I detected a sudden sadness in his voice.

"I knew him personally," he pointed upward.

"Can you see the only thing that mars it?"

"I can see. Yes! Just at the centre of the upper lip on the left hand side."

I saw the gouge where his index finger pointed. Instantly, I noticed that no artisan and tool had caused it. The blemish on the marble ran from the left upper lip to the cheek. I knew then, having seen such scars on the stonework before, that it had been caused by the impact of a bullet.

The disappointment that such a work should have been vandalised must have shown in my questioning expression. The friendly monk nodded, his smile had sorrow in it.

"It is a long story traveller. If you care to abide a while and are interested I will relate it to you?"

"I would not wish to impose on your time or delay you in your devotions."

"You are very considerate for a westerner, my brother. Do not think you waste my time. I have all the eternities and it is a lonely existence here. I would be glad of some company."

"Very well. I am interested of course. How did the statue get despoiled in such a manner?"

"This land," he began, "Has known many conquerors. The golden Horde of Temulchin had ridden through and watered their steppe ponies in the mountain streams. Over the centuries others have come, bandits from the turmoil in China. War, revolution, famine and plague have spilled over our borders; have been our constant companions. The original statue of our Prince was of gold, taken for booty by some obscure warlord. The shrine stood empty for a long time. For no man had the ability or the vision to create another semblance of our Lord Gautama.

Till, one day, a young man; one of two brothers, peasants, workers on the land; came to the notice of the nobility. He was a sculptor, a worker in metal, stone and marble. He created the masterpiece you see before you.

Though as always, peace is a fleeting thing. A shadow fell over the land. New invaders! The Japanese! Our small, ill equipped, but gallant army was overwhelmed and decimated. Our country was overrun by the warriors of Nippon. However, in this mountain vastness remained partisan bands who continued to strive against the yoke of the oppressors. Both brothers led two groups of guerrillas. The one who was an artist laid down chisel and hammer and took up arms in the great struggle. The other, the farmer, had a deformed leg, yet this did not deter him from fighting for freedom.

A small theatre of war it was, ignored in the great campaigns of a global conflict, but important to us, nevertheless.

The years wore on. The war came to an end, peace returned, for a while. Though in human affairs this is always only a respite. The brothers returned home to the accolade of the people."

A bitter smile played around his lips.

"Karma is strange, is it not? That two men who have shared the same womb and are born into earthly life by the same mother can hold very diverse ideas?

The artist, a dreamer by his very nature, had great plans for reform for our country. There would be no poor in the post-war world that he envisaged. Everything would be held in common. With the old nobility, the Mandarins gone, there was hope for a better life.

The other brother worked for a democratic republic with a president and elections. It was inevitable that the siblings and their followers should clash, both supported as they were by powerful outside influences of differing ideologies. The resistance groups they had led had grown into well armed and trained forces. Both sides being fanatical in what they believed.

The artist attempted a coup. It failed. The whole land was plunged into a remorseless civil war. After many months the republican cause began to triumph. The insurgents were defeated in battle after battle. Till, at last, the artist with a few surviving comrades fled deep into the bastion of the mountains. Then, hungry, thirsty, abandoned and alone he came to this very shrine. At midnight, where they had both played as boy; where, too, his greatest artistic endeavour stood within these ancient walls.

He entered, alert, pistol in hand. As his straining eyes penetrated the darkness he espied a figure. Kneeling in solitary prayer at the feet of Gautama. Despite his great caution the artist's foot kicked over an unlit ornamental brazier that fell, and in its falling echoed around the temple.

The figure rose and spun to face him. A revolver flamed and in its flaming revealed the countenance of his brother. His own finger was already lightening on the trigger of his weapon. As he felt the tearing impact of the bullet enter his chest his right arm jerked upward to avoid hitting his brother as the automatic discharged.

The shot hit the face of the Buddha. Then he fell forward in death, a smile upon his lips."

For the first time I realised there were tears flooding the eyes of the gentle old monk.

"So that is the story of the scar upon the face of the Lord Gautama. They raised a statue to the artist you know? It stands in the main square of the capital as a liberator, war hero and martyr.

Not so his brother who lapsed into obscurity. For years he has come before this likeness of Lord Gautama. Praying, fasting, searching for forgiveness to ease his restless spirit. Perhaps when his soul passes on he will know the balm of peace at last."

His voice had descended to a whisper. It was then I noticed the deformed foot within the sandal. He saw me start in realisation.

"Yes!" he concluded. "The artist was my brother."

This is a collection of writing by,

David Killop

Published by Portbank Printworks 2009

Brothers

Two battle weary soldiers are riding home again
Good men they've watched dying good men they have slain
They fought for God and country to win the war their way
One wears Union battledress the other rebel grey.

They fought for God and country, killed and maimed and cried
When men they'd known from so far off homes lay in mud and died
They saw them carried to a grave and quickly covered o'er
Then orders would come down again to go and kill some more.

But now the war is over, the battles have been won
And men from every walk of life have gone to feed the gun
And loved ones left behind them have paid the price of war
The songs are not of battle now but song of war no more.

Two saddle weary brothers are camped down for the night
Across a flickering camp fire each sees the others plight
Was it right to go on fighting to go and kill and maim?
Each knows the answer and is sure that this can't start again.

Those saddle weary brothers ride back to their home town
Very soon they marry and quickly settle down
Soon they have some children and they in turn have more
And all they are producing is more fodder for a war

In World War One and World War Two bugles blared once more
How quick the memory blurred to the slaughter gone before
And then there was Korea and a land called Vietnam
Where killing was improving and no-one gave a damn

For the stuff they feed the guns on is the likes of you and me

It's the thing that they revert to when politicians disagree

So should it ever start again, don't be scared to say

Your kids are staying in today and won't be out to play.

The Lady Elizabeth

Lady Elizabeth Smyth-Copeland had some six months earlier married the very eligible Sir William. He, being sixty-nine, was some forty-two years older than his bride. This somewhat unusual union was the main topic of conversation in the tittle-tattle society circles of the time. Sir William was extremely wealthy and not given to modesty. His lifestyle clearly reflected accumulated prosperity which he unstintingly paraded by his lavish spending on the aforesaid Lady Elizabeth.

This was not lost on his several nieces and nephews who he despised heartily on account of their continued and merciless toadying. I bring this up to make the point that as well as an inordinate level of bewilderment among his friends, his relations had not embraced their uncle's nuptial bliss with any degree of enthusiasm.

Indeed, one such nephew had made it his business to find out more about Lady Elizabeth and discovered, much to his delight, that she was at one time known as Lizzie Morton a singer and dancer of little distinction who flouted her God-given gifts in a music hall of less distinction.

The said nephew was quick to report his findings to uncle William, in the vain hope that divorce would ensue, but was shattered to be told by uncle William that he was well aware of this and added that he found the nephew both tiresome and boring, whereupon he called his strapping blacksmith and his apprentice, giving them each a gold sovereign, demanded they escort the revolting nephew off the estate with instructions that the bruises should not be too obvious.

It was in December of 1890 the London Gazette first muted the 'Mysterious Death of Sir William Smyth-Copeland'. A postmortem revealed there was nothing mysterious about it. Sir William had been well and truly dispatched to his place of judgment by a substantial quantity of poison. The subsequent statement from the police stated that poisoning was the cause of death and left it at that.

Not so the hacks. Several newspapers ran with the story embroidering the details as they thought fit. The alleged poison ranged from arsenic to hemlock while Lady Elizabeth's age was the range of twenty-one to thirty-five. Credence was mainly attributed to The London Gazette, who reported, rather soberly, but correctly, that Lady Elizabeth was the twenty-seven year old wife of Sir William, aged sixty-nine, and that he had died from ingesting rat poison administered in his rare malt whisky. It was the dastardly details contained in the London Gazette that gave weight to their story.

The scoop by the L.G. turned out to be the true account of the murder. The age difference of the couple plus some 'leaked information', presumed to have come from someone within the family had placed Lady Elizabeth in an invidious situation. It was no surprise that, in due course, the L.G. announced 'Lady Elizabeth to stand trial for murder'. The story was sweetened by revelations of her colourful past, much to the horror to all respectable people and the delight of some, not so respectable, within the family.

The trial date approached amid a feeding frenzy of newspaper articles. The chances of Lady Elizabeth getting a fair and unbiased trial appeared most unlikely. However, she was to be defended by the celebrated Sir John Abraham, who had the dubious reputation of saving young society ladies from getting their necks stretched following the sudden and untimely death of husbands; most of whom being wealthy. Lady Elizabeth's choice proved one thing, she knew the form.

The prosecution would be conducted by Mr. Andrew Billings. He had ingratiated himself into the law and order lobby by sending some fourteen men and two women to the gallows, most being penniless, using prosecution devices which, if not outwith the law, came close to it. The choice of this upstart was of some disquiet. He was illegitimate and this sat none too well with the self-styled legal hierarchy who were dismayed that he of all people should be prosecuting a lady. The manner in which he pursued the position of prosecutor was described as improper. The truth of the matter was that the case for the prosecution was so strong that no one else would take it on. Having a lady hanged, regardless of background, could be an embarrassment to the established lawyers.

In preparation, Billings studied the police reports and noted at the time of the poisoning only three people were in the bedroom, being the scene of the crime. The first was Sir William. The report pointed out that suicide was unlikely as it was improbable that Sir William would be so foolish as to ruin a glass of rare fine Scotch whisky by adding poison. Such was his pride in his whisky inventory. The second was a Miss Alice McGregor. The report gave an elaborate narrative of Miss McGregor. She was born in Scotland and at a very early age had provided an exceptional service to all her employers. Suffice is to say she had been in the employ of Sir William for more than forty years during which time she had enjoyed an excellent stipend. Billings surmised this canny Scot would be unlikely to kill the goose that lays the golden eggs; in any event, getting another position at her age would be no easy task. There was only one more in the spotlight - Lady Elizabeth the accused. Billings had a job to do and by all that's holy he would do it.

In March, the 17th to be exact, 1891 the day of the trial of Lady Elizabeth Smyth-Copeland, spouse of the late lamented Sir William Smyth-Copeland, finally arrived.

Billings the prosecutor had taken his place in court and watched as the accused and the defense Sir John Abraham entered and assumed their positions.

The packed court was called to rise as the judge entered. Making a half-hearted bow to the jury, he sat himself down.

And so the stage was set. This was Billing's day, the day he had waited so many years for. He was setting himself against the distinguished Sir John Abraham. Winning this case would make or mar him for the rest of his life. He had to win, there were no half measures. He would follow through with every trick he had ever devised. The weight of responsibility made his head swim, if he were the victor he would no longer be an underdog, he would be the celebrated. His future would be assured.

As Billings was preparing his case so too was the pedantic Sir John Abraham, who like Billings, was not averse to maximising on any avenue which would tilt the outcome to his advantage. During these discussions he pointed out several ways, she should consider of how to present herself to the jury. This was of particular interest to his client whose previous business calling was presenting herself to an audience. It was certainly interesting to her and she listened with seeming enthusiasm, much to Sir John's joy, who had held her hand, now and again, to emphasise certain points. Holding hands was quite pleasurable to the divisive Lady Elizabeth, it was all in the scheme of things. However Lady Elizabeth would set the jury afire in her own way.

When the trial began Miss Alice McGregor, the head housekeeper and general factotum for forty years was the first of only two witnesses who could contribute anything of importance as to the guilt or innocence of the accused.

Questioned by Sir John Abraham, his interrogation followed a line that seemed to imply that Miss McGregor knew more than she was telling. In testimony to the police she stated she always carried Sir William's sleeping draught to his bedroom when he retired for the night.

Invariably this would be a large glass of his favourite malt whisky. It was a custom that continued after the marriage to Lady Elizabeth, pressed on this she added Sir William would quaff the whisky while she waited, after which she would then remove the empty glass. Furthermore she added that, after leaving, Lady Elizabeth would remain in Sir William's bedroom as he liked to see her dancing.

Sir John continued stating categorically that Miss McGregor had ample opportunity and means to dispatch Sir William should she be so inclined and further suggested that such talk of dancing in the bedroom was pure fancy on the part of Miss McGregor.

At this point the judge interrupted proceedings to ask Miss McGregor how she knew of this dancing practice if she had already left the bedroom.

Sir John smiled smugly at the judge's question hoping this could make Miss McGregor out to be a judicious and prolific liar but his face froze when Miss McGregor coolly answered that Lady Elizabeth told her. Without prompting she added that on occasions Lady Elizabeth had said she had to cut her routine short as she was concerned that Sir William may suffer a heart attack; which certain members of the jury could well understand.

A ripple of evocative murmurs ran round the court whereupon the judge, his face red with rage, or excitement, banged his gavel for silence.

It was all becoming very confusing.

In cross examination Billings took the opportunity to ridicule this notion on Miss McGregor's guilt pointing out that Miss McGregor was clearly short of motive. Indeed, he added, as a result of Sir William's untimely departure Miss McGregor had been seeking alternative employment which, at her age, would seem unlikely.

Lady Elizabeth now took the stand. She moved gracefully to her position in the courtroom the eyes of the jury focused on the nice turn of ankle and rather fetching black dress which had been extremely economically cut.

Billings opened by asking Lady Elizabeth if she accompanied Miss McGregor to Sir William's bedroom. Yes she did. Did she remain there after Miss McGregor left?

The judge cautioned Billings on this line of questioning; pointing out that Miss McGregor had left with the empty whisky glass, the empty glass, he reiterated. Billings insisted that his line of questioning would give the court some insight into Lady Elizabeth's character as being slightly exuberant and while she was a very beautiful lady it did not follow that she was a puritan and therefore innocent of this dastardly crime.

Sir John defending, now concerned about this so far unrevealed dancing thing, leapt to object but the judge waved a dismissing hand.

Billings continued. So she had remained after Miss McGregor left. Yes she had. Why did she do this? She smiled flirtatiously to the judge.

"Do I have to answer that embarrassing question m'lord?"

"Yes, I'm afraid so," the judge answered apologetically.

She glared at Billings icily, her eyes drawing him daggers.

"I remained in Sir William's bedroom, as Miss McGregor said, because he liked to see me dance."

Billings took no notice of her anger and sensed there was more to know about this dancing.

The judge intervened at this juncture "Mr. Billings let me ask you. Is all this necessary?"

"I'm afraid so m'lord."

The judge was clearly getting irate. "Well, get on with it."

"Can I ask how you were robed for this performance?" Billings was now smirking.

"You can ask!" screeched the judge, a flash of spittle slanting down his robe.

"But Lady Elizabeth will not answer. I will not have Lady Elizabeth subjected to this type of scrutiny in my court."

Billings looked sheepishly at the judge and realised that his question may have implied that her state of dress may have been somewhat exotic; if at all.

Sir John slowly stirred from his chair.

"If I may m'lord?" Sir John Abraham, defence, now realised the gross error Billings had made in pursuing this and rejoiced in it.

"Of course Sir John," the judge answered.

Sir John addressed Lady Elizabeth.

"In evidence Miss McGregor stated that you danced in Sir William's bedroom. Is that the case?"

"That is correct Sir John."

"Furthermore you had stated to Miss McGregor that you had on occasions left the bedroom thinking Sir William might have taken a heart attack. Is that true?"

"That is true Sir John."

"A heart attack would have been a more natural manner to end Sir William's life, if that was your intention." Sir John Abraham looked around the court making the most of his revelation.

"So!" He exclaimed excitedly. "You probably extended his life by leaving the bedroom!"

The judge nodded knowingly.

In due course and in summing up the judge directed the jury to remember this evidence and bare it in mind.

He then added pointedly, "If Lady Elizabeth had wished to murder Sir William she had the means and opportunity to do so. Who would have known? She would never have had to suffer the indignity of appearing in my court and the pain and suffering brought about by an irresponsible press."

In less than an hour, the jury returned having found Lady Elizabeth not guilty.

Lady Elizabeth was released and subsequently disappeared from the London society haunts. Sir William's great mansion with its contents and its grounds had been sold off. In appreciation of their special services the two blacksmiths, old Tom and his apprentice son young Thomas were handsomely rewarded.

Lady Elizabeth was already proving to be generous with Sir William's estate.

Billings was said to have taken to strong drink. It was even reported that sightings had been made of him in some of the seedier London taverns. It was evident Billings was a broken man.

The epilogue.

It was almost a year after the close of the trial that Sir John Abraham discovered a letter on his breakfast table bearing a strange stamp. The letter had been sent from Jamaica.

He opened it and looked at it. Hardly believing what he read he read it again.

Dear Sir John,

 It's Billings! I'm sure you'll remember me. I'm delighted to say that your letter to Lady Elizabeth has been re-addressed. You will be pleased to know that my mother, Miss McGregor is with me and we are settling in nicely at our new coffee estate. Lady Elizabeth (now Mrs. Billings) sends her regards.

She regrets she could not accept your kind offer of marriage but in view of Sir William's rapid departure, perhaps it was just as well.

The Tree

Scraggy fingers grasp the sky
Their fleshy leaves now long time lost
Returned to earth from whence they came
A fallen crown now dressed with frost.

The tree now naked stands serene
While nature tries with snow to dress
Yet thus disrobed the beauty lingers
The tree is still a tree no less.

On its axis spins the earth
And circumnavigates the sun
Moving to that place in space
From whither summer seasons come.

The buds exploding on the branch
Open up to summer rays
And winter nights are giving way
To longer warmer summer days.

The tree all green in glory now
Reveals to us some greater power
Which we may never understand
Until, perhaps, our final hour.

This is a collection of writing by,

Tommy McBride

Published by Portbank Printworks 2009

The Boatman

One quiet October's night, sitting in the front room, Jamie King was reading some passages from the Bible, not being religious it so happens that he picked up the Bible that was laying on the small table by the bay window, it belonged to his great aunt Mary.

As Jamie was reading, sleep eventually crept up on him and soon he was fast asleep and dreaming. It was a funny dream, he felt as if he was on a boat of some kind, not your modern boat or yacht you see, but the old Egyptian type. Sailing down this vast river, it was very hot and humid; the sweat was trickling down his brow.

Thinking to himself, "What is happening to me?"

Standing inside the small cabin that was in the middle of the boat, Jamie brushed against a small picture that hung on the wall of the cabin. Just then he noticed some engraving behind the picture, it read – '1914 Mary King was here to look for her husband Jake, please God help me'. The engraving looked as if blood was oozing from it.

Jamie puzzled at first, "Could these inscriptions belong to my great Aunt Mary?" That night Jamie slept in a tiny bunk inside the cabin. He had just nodded off, when unknowing to him, a scorpion was crawling up his bed sheets. It stopped right in the centre of Jamie's chest; just then Jamie stirred and came face to face with it looking very menacingly at him. As quick as a flash Jamie brushed it off his chest, onto the floor and picked up his shoe and killed the scorpion. Jamie did not get any more sleep that night. Looking out across the river, Jamie noticed a red mist forming just above the water, "Strange," he thought, it seems to be following their boat. The red mist creeps closer to them, suddenly it's all around the boat and fear starts to creep in! The hair on Jamie's neck starts to rise, nervous was Jamie! He could not see a thing ahead of him, and then from nowhere a beastly looking figure was standing right in front of him. At first it looked like a man just standing there, but as the mist started to lift Jamie saw what looked like a jackal's head, a man's torso, long arms and hands that looked like huge claws! Just then, it spoke, "What are you doing here?" it roared out, hot breath blowing from its nostrils, as it ran its claws over Jamie's head.

Jamie stood very still not trying to show his fear, "I don't know," he said. "I just woke up on this boat, in the middle of this river."

The beast starts to talk, "This here river is mine, no living person travels on this boat or river, not unless it's time for them to come!"

Jamie was getting really scared, "It's time for me to wake up," he thought, still thinking how to get out of this dream as it's getting too real for him to believe!

Again the beast speaks, "You have until the fork in the river to choose young man."

"Choose what?" Jamie said.

"Life or Death," the beast replied, piercing Jamie's arm with its claw, blood started to ooze out of Jamie's left arm, the beast held up its claw to its mouth tasting young Jamie's blood, licking its lips with its horrible blue tongue, then as quick as it came, it disappeared into thin air.

Jamie's mind was racing, shouting, "Wake up, wake up!"

But to Jamie's regret, he was still standing there in the middle of the boat, "God help me, what is happening to me?"

Jamie sat down holding his head in his hands; he looked across the floor, and saw a book of some sort, stuck under his bunk bed. Jamie picked up the book and started to read the first page. It read – 'This here diary belongs to Mrs. Mary King!'

Page after page, Jamie read from start to finish. It told of Jamie's aunt coming to Cairo looking for her husband Jake, who was an archaeologist, looking for some lost Pharaoh's tomb, and how she has searched high and low for him, but to no avail!

Jamie was indeed intrigued by the last two pages of the diary, it read, 'Here on the River Nile, the second of October 1914, the crew is getting scared about a red mist that is following us. Still can't find Jake, it's been two months now.' Jamie reads on, 'I had a bad dream last night, red mist all around us, then a large beast appeared, with a jackal's head and says "I am the Boatman"' - the last part of the page is not complete, it stopped at – 'woke up this morning and the crew was gone, the boat seems to be approaching a fork in the river!'

Jamie felt a cold shiver running down his spine! "It's my dream, that's in that diary, but how can that be?" Night creeps back in, Jamie, looking out down the river, there about a mile ahead of him he saw what looked like an island with two large palm trees "Strange," he thought, then it hit him, "Bloody hell it's the fork in the river!"

The red mist suddenly appears, forming around the boat.

Jamie looks around for some kind of weapon to defend himself with, but all he could find was a metal pole that the crew used to dock that boat. Just then the beast appeared right in front of Jamie!

"Well young man, what is it to be - Life or Death?" Jamie moved with great speed and tried to spear the beast, but to it's satisfaction he missed. "Ha! Ha!" it laughed. "At last you have chosen death, Jamie King. I'm the Boatman, the beast of Satan; I take the souls of others." It swung its large claw, which hit Jamie in his side, ripping it open. Jamie felt the pain, burning and soaring to his brain!

He was lying on his back, looking at the great beast staring at him, ready to take his soul from him.

After the great battle they just had, the beast rose up ready to strike the final blow. Jamie raised the pole straight up hoping the beast would fall down onto the point of it, which to Jamie's joy, the last thing he heard was the banishing howl that the beast let out of its body as the pole went straight through its chest.

The clock struck midnight in the front room, Jamie rubbing his eyes, sweat running out of his body. He looks on the floor, there lies his aunt's Bible, Jamie picks it up and puts it on the small table. "God that was some dream," he thought to himself.

Feeling cold, Jamie went to the fire to put more logs on. Just then he felt a warm feeling down his side, Jamie looked down to see a large gash on his side, the marks a claw had made? Jamie reached to rake the fire with the metal poker and to his surprise there was blood dripping off the end of it. Quickly, he went back to the armchair by the window and picked up the Bible. He flicked through it with great speed, "Nothing there," he said to himself. Looking down on the floor, Jamie sees a bookmarker; he picks it up and reads it. 'Thank you Jamie for killing the beast. Your uncle and I lived on till nineteen-thirty, we had a happy life, thanks to you.'

Songs of Innocence

Strips of willow, blowing in the wind, jackdaws cawing from
The skies, church bells ringing and little children stepping in,
Their voices like a song of innocence.
Dark thoughts and terrible dreams, run through his mind.
He stands, contemplating of what he has done,
He knows his time is coming, listening to songs of innocence.
People rushing, pushing, oblivious of what they are doing.
The songs of innocence echo from the church,
People shout, "Hang him, hang him"
For they cannot hear the songs of innocence.
Soon the nightmares will stop, little angels will come to him,
He knows now what he has done,
Madness, a terrible madness, lurking in him.
That terrible morning, as he awoke, his hands
Around the child's throat. People did not listen, to his innocence.
Before he knows the trapdoor opens, the crowd stops shouting,
Deadly hush, as he swings upon the gallows.
The last thing he hears is little children singing the songs of innocence?

A Little Boy Lost

"Hear ye! Hear ye!" the town crier yelled,

Carrying in the wind, his voice did ring.

"A little boy lost

In the snow and frost," he did yell.

The people shouted,

"Where? Where? Where?"

"In Delaware Wood! In Delaware Wood!"

Came his hoarse reply, the people did multiply.

Let's search the neighbourhood,

He must be nearby.

Deep snow! Deep snow! Moon shining down,

Bells were ringing in the town, more snow falling down.

Ground was rock hard, let's search barns and yards.

A farmer shouts, "Here!" leaping in the dark.

Father and Mother cry joyfully, the people shout jovially,

Little boy amid sheep, oblivious and asleep.

Ella

Ella, Oh Ella, walking on sands so fine.
Tides turn, with every step you take,
Your hair shines like the moon above.
Casting imprints of love, for all to see.

Ella, Oh Ella, standing tall.
Body like a camellia,
Blooming out,
You blossom, for all.

Smell and feel that cool, sea breeze, blowing in.
Holding hands, watching stars cascading across,
Dark blue heavens, with eyes that twinkle like
Diamonds, the love for you I hold within.

Holding On

Grandfather, Grandfather, sleeping in your old chair.
The smell of black twist, still lingers in the air.
Hands of granite, but gentle to the touch.
In my dreams, I miss you so much.

In my dreams, I once believed.
The house, the house, does no-longer stand.
Just a space, a vacuum of grace.
Visions of happiness, memories are retrieved.

Tired eyes, looking into dark extinction.
The smell of varnish, seeps from the walls.
Grained woodwork does cover it all.
In my dreams, you did lack conviction.

In my dreams, generations of brood
Allowed brick walls, to weep of change.
Your presence of time, is sadly missed.
Bringing conclusion to adulthood.

Generations, of a lifetime passes, yes you were so grand.
Standing tall, behold, those tired, steely-grey eyes!
My time has come, to let you go.
But in my dreams, I take your hand.

Memories

Like taking a trip back in time, ash pathways, neat trimmed grass.
Faces clear as day, time ebbing away, reflections of an hourglass.
Smell of fresh cut flowers, drifting in the light evening breeze.
The young man walking on the pathway, carrying his valise.

Memories flooding his mind, tormenting his present time.
He quickly brushes the canvas, to show the paradigm.
The scent of jasmine inspires him to create a prime painting
Of walks with his Mother, in the summertime.

Grand polished stones of marble, stand tall in a row.
Some with gold-coloured letters, to show their status quo.
Like a pathway to heaven, they're spread over the ground.
His mind and thoughts, try to expound.

Swallows going to and fro, skylarks in blue skies soaring.
Here he sits under the yew tree, pencils and brushes ready.
Hours of dedication, to accomplish his commission.
Memories, dreams, do come, while the birds were sleeping.

His equanimity starting to settle, no more demented nightmares.
He remembers the terrible workhouse, voices echoing beware.
Tiny boy in bed, sweating, crying and praying for answers.
He tries to blank those terrible memories, demons advancing.

His mother cried that terrible day, when officials took him away.
Father dead, Mother, too ill to look after a little boy, it's arrogating.
Years past, Mother and son reunited, they leave without delay.
Mother would say, "Just like your Father, always painting."

Looking at the old granite headstone, sitting under the yew tree.

Alberto the crazy painter people called as they passed by.

Peace at last Mother, demons gone, wouldn't you agree?

Say hello to Father, as Alberto's going bye-bye.

Mermaid Fantasy

Listen, listen, can you hear it?
That gentle, gentle, lapping sound.
The tide, the tide, is coming ashore,
Bringing the fresh smell from the sea.

My head, it rests on driftwood.
Listening and dreaming,
She suddenly appears,
Like a spirit on the wind.

Her glowing red hair,
Like a burning sun.
Skipping, dancing on the sand,
She floats, upon the air.

I reach, but behold, I can't touch.
She's so real. The sea spray,
Dances on her skin.
A fantasy, I say, but look her footprints,
Are being washed away.

Ripples

The tide causes it,
The water makes it,
Flowing freely it leaves
Its mark every day.

Smooth seas, rough seas,
Storm, it is still the same,
Miles and miles of it.

We walk on it, we look at it,
We can't see how the sea causes it, but
Every day is the same, it looks like
An article of wonder of the world.
It's simple, the moon rules it.

The tide goes out, there's miles
Of it, we look and see a desert
Of sand, but it's wet and soft to
Walk on, sit back and look at it.
What is it? Ripples and ripples of sand.

This is a collection of writing by,

Preston McGlone

Published by Portbank Printworks 2009

Bumble-Knee

My Auntie Nellie, took not well
John, took her up to Tunbridge Wells
Is Tunbridge Wells, no' in Dundee?
It is but listen, wait and see
Hear me out, please do not scoff
John went up, to play some golf

The crafty bugger telt his maw
After she had, had her faw
The best place maw, for you to be
Is up there yonder, in Dundee
Tunbridge Wells, is the place to be
Doctor, doctor look and see
Is there something wrong wae ma maw's knee?

See that woman over there
Sittin' in the plastic chair
She's away with the fairies
She's never in, oops,
Is that pish runnin' down ma shin?

Big Tam came tae cut the grass
And said you can stick the money on a horse
Buy a horse did Ah hear you say?
Then I'll hiv-tae buy it bloody hay

Naw! The money put it on a horse
The money, honey! Said Big Tam
Buy some honey wae the money?
Said Auntie Nell
Would it no' then all, turn to jell?

The quack, the sawbones in Dundee
Said it was her kid-in-ee
Glasgow bound you'll have to be
Down to the Royal Infirmare-e

Where they will weigh you, and display you
On x-ray charts, for all to see
Doctors fiddle about, and fart around
Keep Mrs. Ferguson, on the ground

We have to look and wait some more
They send her up to the fourth floor
Prod and poke, then, we'll look and see
If it is that, bloody knee

Auntie Ellen, you ain't looking good!
Are you eating this hospital food?
You know this stuff will make you ill
They make it out of old pig swill

Cousin Lizzy said tae John
Ah think she wants tae ho'd yir hawn
She's feeling lowly, she's feeling poor
That yin there's a right auld holy roller

Always rattlin' them holy beads
She prays and prays to do good deeds
She said a prayer for all to please
Offered one up for ma sore knees

Every week they come to see
If the doctor's fixed that bloody knee
The knee's ok it's feeling numb
Do you think it's caused by ma sore bum?

My sore bum now there's a thing
Does this goony show aff, ma ding-a-ling
Ma Nancy Pretty, that special thing
When the doctor goes there, I start to sing
The poor nurses think I'm aff ma heid
But Nancy Pretty is a special need

John and Frances come every day
Along Glasgow's roads they make their way
Come rain or shine and hell's high snow
John and Frances just had to know
Had they got it fixed, and was it dun?
Was the healing cream on Nell's bum?

Blisters and sores they came to see
They didn't give a F about Nell's sore knee
They came for laughter and for fun
To rub the cream on Nellie's bum

Whit about ma leg Nell said
Ah canny get it oot the bed
Bring the hoist, and lift me up
And don't be lookin', at ma butter cup
It once was yellow, shining bright
Now you can't see it for the sugerallie water I must sip

Celebrity status, she had become
They came from far and wide, to see Nell's bum
They flew across from countries far
To get their fingers in the jar
The ointment, the cream the hallowed healer
Preston wanted just to feel her

Betty crossed the ocean green
To see this thing, she had never seen
Ah came as quickly as I could
When she saw Nell's leg she understood
Doctor! Nurse! Can you tell me more?
Ah'm worried sick, ah'm tae the door

Don't you worry don't you fret
We've never lost tae a scaddied bum, yet
We'll turn Nell over, on her tum
And apply the cream tae her sore bum

Rose and Ian came from Bearsden, posh!
The first thing they said was oh my gosh!
Oh my goodness gracious me,
We'll call the doctor for to see
Naw! Naw, Rose it's ok, Ah telt the

Doctor no tae worry
Ma nephew's comin', young Ian Murray
Ah told the nurses that he would come
Ian son, grab the cream, and rub ma bum

Ellen's sister, Elizabeth, travelled from Perth afar
She too had heard of this pure magic stuff. Miracles in a jar
The ointment! The cream! The mira-coil!
Something like Lorenzo's Oil
It cures the sick, and heals the lame
Heals sores like you would never think
But it's keeping down an awful swelling

Nicola came with Betty, that's Nick's ma
To Phil her da and Tony her man, she waved them bye ta-ta
Ah'll take the weans wae me an' ma ma
An' Ah'll bid yae both ferwell
We're goin' doon tae Glesga toon
Tae visit ma sick Auntie Nell

Liz my sister says, they've moved my Auntie Nell
To somewhere really good
Lightburn, by the Carantyne, and feed them
Lovely food
The Serpentyne and the Carantyne that sounds
Really royal, perhaps that's where they got
The cream like yon Lorenzo's Oil

Good news and bad news Nell this is a royal day

The doctor said the leg's ok

The bad news we must have, sorry Nell

My darling dear the bum is coming aff.

Dead Write

Who are these men lying bleeding and dead?
In the field red soaked with blood
Beneath the white-hot sun
The scribe, the scholar with intellect
A man without a gun.

He wrote of heroes' guts and gore
Of fearless bravery
Of selfless acts beyond belief
On the battlefields of woeful grief.

He pencilled in the deaths of men
The efforts that they made
With rasping, gasping, dying breath
The things that must be said.

Wounded here on a battlefield
Fallen comrades all around
Shell-shocked, shot and blown to bits
Coughing, rasping, gasping now
In spasmodic jerking fits
By the gas they did emit

The orders came from down the line
Fags out, fix bayonets, steady son
Soon it will be time
For you to go up and over
For to receive your coat of lime

Mother, father, darling wife
My beautiful children dear
When I think of you my family
For the war I have no fear

Brave soldiers wait in silent prayer
The whistle for to blow
Some shuffle, scuffle, stamp their feet
Up and over they must go

First or last, slow or fast
It didn't really matter
In no-man's-land you're on your own
With thousands to the slaughter

Dismembered bodies fall to the ground
Soldiers cry with pain and moan
Sitting in puddles of blood and guts
Shell-shocked to the core

"Up and at them," came the battle cry
As the officer passed them by
"Up and at them," came the battle cry
As he took one in the eye

To the ground mixed
With mud and blood he fell
The brave officer lay there still
Up, over and onwards he had went
And now he lay there killed

They died in battle

Which was all in vain

The scribe he was also slain

He had come to war without a gun

Or a rifle in his hand

He came to write for you and me

And to die in no-man's-land.

Forgive

A seat of learning for those that give
A pause of rest for those that sing
They pass on peace through prayer and hymn
A golden throne for God our king

Please Lord forgive me a wicked sinner
I never thought I would be a winner
Mindless misdeeds and acts so grim
I weaved a web of my own gin

To catch and trap pull tight and snare
Ruthless acts without a care
Souls stained black, tinged full of sadness
I pray to God for light and gladness

Forgiveness from a higher power
Cleanse my soul of sin and badness
Let me right the wrongs I did
Please Lord God most spiritually divine
Let sinning ways no longer be mine.

March to Hell

Tombs and vaults of waiting dead
Stand at the gates in mournful dread
Hearses filled with more dead souls
Their names are marked in blooded scrolls

Written on the devil's stone
That shadows cast, the ugly reading of our past
Reading good or looking bad
The mourners bow their heads and sigh

Corpses march and souls they fly
Confusion comes for those who die
Death has come it's so profound
Prepare the earth and dig the ground
With the caravan your soul be found
On desolate plains which are unsound

Bound and chained you march together
Across the plains of forgotten time
Your souls are lost to God forever
Bloody chains on rusty feet
Make a chime of crushed defeat

One so vain and full of pride
No rest for the wicked no place to hide
Forgotten time the winds of change
Have washed you up on death's dark tide

Souls they fly and corpses march
Looking for some marble arch
For to cool them in its shadows cast
On this plain of pain and desolation parched

Water for these sorrowful souls would be
A merciful conciliation
It's guarded by the demon hounds
On the plains of desolation

Lifeless, still, stood eerie trees
Upright motionless in the breeze
Clothed cold, in peeling withering bark
They shone with dimness in the dark
Long dead branches pointed east
Along this path you'll find the beast

Undertakers dressed in rags
Line the path with mournful hags
Next to one who screwed you down
Before they put you in the ground
Laughing, mocking, sickening sounds
Creeps along graveyards hallowed grounds

Along the path stood countless headstones
Above open graves lay sun-bleached bones
Shuffling down the track with fear
Knowing that the beast was near
Closer as they onwards tread
Filled with woeful depths of dread

Looking back in lamentable sorrow

Take note and notice of no tomorrow

Anger, bitterness, fear and hate

The time has come to meet your fate

No need to knock or ring the bell

You're standing at the gates of hell.

Please God

Oh! Please God! Save us in our hour of need.
I pray for you to intercede
Hear our plead gracious loving king
The Lord almighty that sees all things.

Don't let us be the ones you miss
Touch us with your heavenly bliss
With love for thee your feet we kiss
In hope we pray for your return
Save us, heal us or in hell we burn

We come to you our hearts laid bare
To you the king our souls to spare
Peace of mind, understanding love
We know it comes from you above

From there in heaven, not far away
Come to our hearts Lord and in our
Hearts Lord, please just stay
Save our souls, don't let us stray.

Thank you, Father.

The Bells of Hell

Enter welcome come on in
Are those your morals that you bring?
The church of demented practice sings
Sell your soul do your thing

Snare the souls of careless young
In adulthood the work is done
Trapped in endless indecision
Leave it for the inquisition
Can they, will they, have they killed?
Did they do it of their own free will?

You paced the floor with anxious haste
This life was squandered what a waste
Many crossroads we did meet
The choice was yours to change your fate
Heads you win tails too late

Fiends and demons and bogeymen
Dark creatures of the night
Swoop down with talon claws
Crushing flesh and bone of wretched souls
Monstrous demons in errant flight

Ding dong the bells rang out warning
For those who are in doubt
Hobgoblins and trolls what creep about
Looking for some souls lost out

Rampant evil spirits fly endless
On errant wing
Waiting for your soul now dead
Down to hell far below
Your souls, now they must bring

Rat-shaped, cat-like creatures and demon
Dogs of stealth slink around the table legs
Ripping rotting flesh from unsuspecting
Banquettes dining on the dead

Horror gory bloodied flesh a banquette
For the dead
Suffering souls around the table sit
Waiting to be fed

Red, mushy, pulp of flesh and bone
Rotten human meat, trampled by innumerable souls
With festered flesh on feet
Damned and sorrowful hell-bound trudging
With moaning sound
Deep down in the bowels of hell
There they will be found

Human wants for your soul did sell
No turning back to make amends
Your chances came good fortune spent
Too late to pray you can't repent
Regret and sorrow you now feel
Abandon hope all who enter here
The bells of hell, for you, now peel

This is a collection of writing by,

Kenny McGuigan

Published by Portbank Printworks 2009

The Examination

A big fat wummin with a most serious complaint
Went doon tae the doctor's because she felt faint,
"Oh doctir, it's ma piles," she was forced to admit
"They're that biddy sair, that Ah can't even sit!"

So aff tae the hospital he duly did send her
Tae consult wi' a surgeon who could possibly mend her,
She stood all the way on the bus intae town
'cause the size of her piles meant she couldnae sit down.

She arrived at the hospital and went in the door
Then got on the lift up tae Ward 44.
The place was all quiet with no-one in sight
When out stepped a man, dressed all in white.

"Gonnae look at ma piles for they're givin' me jip?"
She said tae the man with a tremor of lip.
"Step intae ma office, it's just over here."
And they entered a room marked Doctor A. Greer

"Bend over that table tae Ah see whit is wrong,"
And he examined her thoroughly, but didnae take long.
"Will ye dae me a favour and see Mr Shore?
He's at the end of the corridor, in room 54."

Embarrassed but grateful she then made her way
Worried and anxious about what Shore might say.
She opened the door and she asked Mr Shore
Tae look at her piles, which were awfully sore.

"Ah see whit ye mean, hen," he curtly exclaimed
"They're swelt up and bleedin' and very inflamed.
"Wid ye go see ma colleague, Mr Tam Cook?
He's in room 59 and wid be keen for a look."

In room 59, a man dressed in white
Looked over his glasses and welcomed the sight.
"Mr Cook is ma name," he formally declared
She bent over the table and he hummed as he stared.

"These piles are massive," Tam Cook proclaimed
"They're black and they're hingin' and very inflamed
I've never seen anything like it before,
In the name of God, they look terribly sore."

"Dae ye think ye can help me?" the fat wummin pleaded
"Well, it's gonnae be hard," Mr Tam Cook conceded,
"Ye'd best see a doctor who'll know whit tae do
You see we're just the painters, sent by the broo!"

A Toast

I watch as Mr. Big takes the good things of life
Me? Well I'll just have to wait
I go ask the preacher, who is also the teacher
And he tells me it is just my fate.
It's a spiritual fight that is killing me
But Mr. Big has his aims and his goal,
Just don't talk to me about my being free
When Mr. Big is in total control.

So let's drink a toast to you, Mr. Big
To the owner of my body's sweat
My brew tastes a little more bitter than yours
But it may turn out different yet.
Hurrah for the man who is wearing a suit
That costs more than he pays me a wage
His wallet in bulging yet my belly's rumbling
I am old but we're both the same age.

My work makes him wealthy, his children are healthy
Mine? Well they could do with more
When I asked for a pay rise to help us get by
He felt I deserved nothing more
I could tell by his eyes and that look of surprise
He was ready to show me the door
The gel in his hair and the scent that he wears
Costs more than he pays me for sure.

So let's drink a toast to you, Mr. Big
To the owner of my body's sweat
My brew tastes a little more bitter than yours
But it may turn out different yet.
Hurrah for the man who is wearing a suit
That costs more than he pays me a wage
His wallet in bulging yet my belly's rumbling
I am old but we're both the same age.

His wife has arrived and it's five fifty five
Mine? She's a lady and more
The sweat-master's wife who seems so full of life
Is cosmetic and false to the core
On reflection I see that it's better being me
Than a man who is vain and obsessed
'cause it's my victory and in all reality
I know who lives their life best.

So let's drink a toast to you, Mr. Big
You're the owner of my body's sweat
But my spirit is strong, it refuses to yield
And things will be different yet.
Keep all your fuss it will all turn to dust
You have built your foundations in sand
Truth and integrity. Love, hope and loyalty
Words that you don't understand.

Ah Wanna Be A Cowboy!

Ah'm gonna wear big cowboy boots; tie a hanky roon ma neck
Eat baked beans, slap ma thigh and holler "What the Heck!"
Cowboys had a great old time, they always got their girl
Their names were always Duke or Kid; but never, ever, Cyril.

Cause Ah wanna be a cowboy; the fastest gun in town
Ah'll chew a lump of nicotine and always wear a frown

Ah'll go an' buy a big old horse and call him Crazy Darnit
An' Ah'll wear a Marshall's badge an' Ah'll round up all the varmints
Ah'll learn lasso and on ma chin Ah'll grow a three- day stubble
Then Ah'll patrol round Airdrie town; lookin' for trouble

Cause Ah wanna be a cowboy; the fastest gun in town
Ah'll chew a lump of nicotine and always wear a frown

But their aint no call for cowboys in dear old Airdrie town
Though some guys do wear cowboy boots and most put on a frown
And there aint no place to park yer horse down there at Airdrie Cross
You cannae even park yer car; the place is such a loss

Cause Ah wanna be a cowboy; the fastest gun in town
Ah'll chew a lump of nicotine and always wear a frown

So Ah'll never be a cowboy; and Ah'll never get the girl
Ah guess Ah'll just have to keep on bein' plain old handsome Cyril.

Chucklet Hut Academy was the worst school in the district. Any teacher under the age of thirty-five was either a pin up or an alien. On one of my rare appearances there I once heard a history teacher called Mr. McEvan ask, "When the English invaded Scotland, what did they come in?" There was a long silence as Mr. McEvan stood there, his eyebrows raised so high they were in danger of disappearing over the horizon of his bald eggy head. He cupped his hand to his ear expectantly. "Anyone?" His toothbrush moustache pouting as his lips pursed. Big Staffy up the back stopped munching on his Curly Wurly long enough to call out, "Chariots, Sir."

McEvan's face crumpled in exasperation. "No, boys! Hordes, boys! They came in hordes."

I have always enjoyed learning. My problem at school was that the teachers at The Chuckle were pretty hopeless at communicating. Just when I thought I'd learned something. I'd discover I was wrong. I was eleven before I discovered I didn't know the proper words to the Lord's Prayer. I used to recite, "Hallow be Thy name, Thy ding dong dung..." Throughout my school experience I was misunderstood and I misunderstood teachers. Why didn't they make learning fun? It seemed to me that most of them were going through the motions - but it was even more complicated for me. You've probably heard the old music hall routine when the clippie (as bus conductors were known) tells a passenger, "Come on, get aff". My education was like that. Yet there was an air of primitive innocence about the communication breakdown. The bus conductor was sending a contradictory message, obviously, but every Scot will know exactly what she meant. Same with Mr. McEvan. Once the initial crossed wires were sorted we all knew that he did not want us to tell him the mode of transport the English used, but the descriptive words to show that the English came in huge numbers and with great ferocity, as the term 'hordes' suggests. He might well have called them massive battalions.

These days communication is manipulated in a far more sinister way than ever before. If we are not quite living in an Orwellian society then we are not far off it. Politics and business are by far the biggest offenders in the art of miscommunication. George Bush proclaimed 'Mission Accomplished' two years ago in Iraq. The day before I wrote this the three thousandth US soldier had been killed there, and 665,000 Iraqi civilians in total were dead. 'Spin' has become the order of the day everywhere. Failure = Success. Lies = Truth. And, like George Orwell wrote in his classic book '1984', 'Ignorance is Strength' and 'Slavery is Freedom'. Age Concern predicted 15,000 Scottish old age pensioners will die this winter due to hypothermia. They will die because they cannot afford to heat their homes. Some crusty old reactionary appeared from his country pile and advised the elderly to wear hats and gloves, and remember to eat hot soup while promoting the goodness of porridge. My papa said this sort of rhetoric reminded him of the 'hungry thirties' as the depression in world capitalism was known. Papa said the toffs used to write letters in to the papers complaining that while some people claimed to be poor, many were putting a dollop of jam on their bread!

Like many people these days I have a television which allows me to view a multitude of channels. Recently, I was slumped on the chaise-longue watching a dramatisation of Charles Dicken's 'A Tale of Two Cities'. It is most certainly one of the best works ever written. However, the ruling elite of those days did not care much for the classic. Most of Europe was in revolutionary fervent at the time, and the 'hordes' (as McEven would have called them) were wasting no time in stringing up kings and dukes by their fat necks. The participants of the Great French Revolution did exactly that. One cannot begin to imagine the horrors of trying to survive in the period leading to the revolution. Foulon, a great Duke and close confidant of the King had said of the French masses, "If they have no bread, they can eat grass." Later, Foulon was found dangling from a rope, his mouth stuffed with turf in one of history's ironies.

Dickens had written 'A Tale of Two Cities' as a result of the contrasts in society he was witnessing. "They were good times, they were bad times," he wrote. The poor were without hope. Starvation, disease and want were rife. Death was but a day away. Infants were born, lived and died without ever having had anything to eat. On the other side of the same society, the privileged and the wealthy lived idyllic lives, far removed from the grinding poverty of the masses. As I watched the interpretation of the story it became clear that there was an underlying message. In short it was that the Revolution in France was a bad thing and that kings, queens and an elite hierarchy was and is good. At one point in the amateurish production some leaders of the French Revolutionary movement appeared, determinedly cast as the villains of the piece. Shadowy figures, faces twisted with anger and hate shouting things like, "Down with zee King", emerged from the shadows, menacingly. Some had limps, others had humphs on their backs.

And according to the production of the television play, London's taverns were doing a roaring trade. The poor women were portrayed as coarse, buxom, bar-flies, saying in a craggy cockney voice to the gentlemen in nicely tailored capes and hats, "Cor, mister, you've got a big un. A cane I mean..." as the wench perched herself on his knee. It was part Oliver Twist the pantomime and part Carry On Up the Eiffel Town film. Men covered in grime drank greedily from tankards frothing with ale. If Norman Tebbit had been around at the time he'd have been giving an interview to Sky News along the lines, "This proves that ASBO's (Anti-Social Behaviour Orders) are the correct way to proceed. These people are feigning poverty, they certainly can find the money to drink!" A Tony Blair led Labour opposition would have opposed ASBO's on the grounds that it was an attack on civil liberties and merely an attempt to paper over the cracks of the social ills causing society's problems and further stigmatisation of the poor. Well, Charles Dickens' book was a sensation and is still widely read today. In this, the first decade of the 21st century, when the world has never known such wealth and the gap between rich and poor has never been wider, politicians tell us we've never had it so good! In an OPEC report commissioned to show the state of the conditions in the developed western economies, Britain trailed in last of twenty-one countries examined. The US, our friends across the Atlantic, finished just ahead of us in twentieth place. The problem was that Dickens saw the solution as being as increase in altruism and increased charity. The ruling horde must have breathed a great sigh of relief, because across the channel in France, Robespierre, Danton and Marat had drawn different conclusions and stormed the Bastille before eventually seeing the revolution through; abolishing the monarchy and with it the system of nepotism and privilege which drew France into a new age as a modern republic.

Communication. Who needs it?

First Confession

The great day had nearly arrived. All the eight year-olds from the parish of St Barney's, hell bound and bloated with sin, were to make their first confession. I had practised carefully in the lead up to this most blessed event. I was desperate to denounce my depraved and sinful ways. I was also very worried; for just the week before, the Ma had been very angry after I stole Paddy McGrory's bogey, then crashed it into the side of Peggy O'Keefe's shop at the bottom of the hill. This was one of the reasons I was in need of the Sacrament. The Ma said Paddy hadn't stopped greetin' ever since. In a desperate attempt to steer clear of Lucifer's Gates I had, just the Monday before, handed over no less than a shiny shilling to the Black Babies. This honourable self-sacrifice would surely not have been missed by the Holy Ghost. My sterling donation had meant my card was completed and I could name the Black Baby whose miserable life would change irreversibly because of my good deed. I wanted to call the benefactor Errol, after Errol Flynn the movie star, but even in my young mind, I had an inkling that this title might cause some form of indignant angst in Miss Nicol, my musky smelling teacher. So I changed it to Patrick; that would please her. In the back of my mind, I recalled the hammering inflicted on my best pal Pidge when he insisted on calling twins "The Righteous Brothers", and to this very day, I wonder how John, Paul, George and Ringo, or Sonny and Cher for that matter, are getting on in a village near Dodoma, in the scorching African sun.

Pidge was more excited than me. While I hoped for unconditional, holy release from my world of selfish hedonism, the bold Pidge saw the occasion solely as a means to enrich himself. He had been saying for over a week, "Everybody gie's ye money. Everybody gie's ye money". Pidge had an understanding of the mysterious ritual having been well tutored by his two older brothers. Being the eldest in my family, I had to rely on the Ma and Da for information. The Ma said it was a great honour, a glorious chapter in God's Book of Life. This had a disconcerting effect on me and I became preoccupied about God who would surely be writing all the bad things about me. The Ma said the Holy Ghost was everywhere and could see everything that everybody ever done. I hoped he had been looking the other way every second Saturday when Pidge and our gang sneaked into the Regal picture house. I had a riddy on just thinking about it. This was one of the reasons I hadn't written my sins down anywhere, preferring to store the list in my head. I would need to tell Father O'Malley that I habitually stole whelks off the big fat moustachioed lady who had a stall at the fountain. The Ma said if you stole, that was it, you went straight before the throne of Lucifer himself - no Purgatory, nothing. "Straight down ye will go," she told me. Well, the only way to avoid such a calamity was to pray (in earnest) to Saint Gerard Majella, the friend of the poor and the workers. Saint Gerard Majella must have been sick listening to me.

The day itself started in disaster. We slept in. I was dunted awake by the Ma who was running around saying what she always said when we slept in, "Not a wean washed and the French fleet in port." Then to add tension to the drama, my hair was sticking up and no amount of water, rubbing, or the Ma licking it would flatten it close to the head. The remedy was the carbolic soap and the guilty tuft was finally combed into submission. The Da was still in because it was his back-shift week at the strip mill. The Ma scolded my unruly hair, "May Our Lady of Perpetual Succour forgive ye." I stood guilty before the Holy Mother of having a cow's lick. "When Blessed John Ogilvie wis getting hisel' executed fur ye at Glasgow Cross..." the Ma's petition was cut short by a strong smell of burning. Our Angela burnt the toast she was supposed to be watching.

All the penitents were guided to their pews like lambs to the slaughter, and Miss Nicol instructed us in hushed but assertive tones to establish the contact with God, a necessary prerequisite to receipt of the Blessed Sacrament. I tried so hard that when I eventually opened my eyes I was seeing stars and everything was blurred. Pidge said I looked as if I was doing a jobby. I promised God, Our Lady, the Holy Ghost, Saint Gerard Majella and all the martyrs that I would never talk to Pidge again. As far as I was concerned, talking about a jobby just when you have decided to be holy for the rest of your life was a mortal sin. The butterflies in my stomach were certainly flying as it got nearer my turn. Pidge was immediately before me. Then an odd thing happened. I found myself being drawn against my will to eavesdropping on the sins of others. It was easy to hear the goings on, especially with big Father O'Malley having the booming deep voice. But is there not surely something wrong with straining the head handles so as to earwig on the transgressions of others.

My turn came and I stepped nervously towards the big, imposing door of the mystery box. My eyes had to adjust to the dark. I could see the auld Father right enough, well, his outline, behind a black lace mesh. Would he recognise me? This quick mental appraisal left me with short-term memory malfunction. I told the Lord's mediator about the theft of Paddy's bogey, how I cursed twice at Sully, for his lack of talent as a footballer meant he kept kicking the ball over the wall into Starey-eye Green's garden, and old Starey-eye never gave us our ball back. "And is that all, my child?" asked the loudhailer only inches from me. So I told him the Ma had told me anything else was a matter for a lawyer. "Say three Hail Marys and a Glory Be. Go now and sin no more." I went to the back of the chapel, head held high in my new found spiritual well-being. Brother Doris of the Marist Brothers said that if you had the misfortune to be mangled under the wheels of a tram, The Blessed Sacrament of Confession ensured you would go straight to heaven. I said my penance in my best earnest manner and looked to Pidge. Clearly, his sinning had been more serious than mine. It served him right for taking about jobbies in God's House. When everyone did emerge, some were clearly more affected than others. The girls especially, were saying they felt completely different. Emelia Sprok was one such blether, and predictably, Brian Mirthy would not be outdone. Father had been so impressed by Mirth's impeccable First Confession, he was going to tell the Bishop about it! Poor Mirth, even after all these years he hasn't changed a bit. He joined the police force when he relished his role in battering striking miners taking lawful action to protect their jobs and their communities and a way of life. Still, Mirth wasn't affected - that was always his mentality. When we were about twelve years old Mirth played with all the younger boys, and as a group we didn't care much for the way he manipulated them. Our crowd saw him as a bit of a joke. His mother used to steal money from an elderly neighbour, so we steered well clear of him. I could tell this burned away at him, whenever our paths did cross, though this was very few and far between. But we can all sleep sound in our beds at night, because the Mirth man is on the case. Indeed he has been promoted to high office!

Half a lifetime has passed since that encounter at Saint Barney's and my experience of the strange occurrence. So what do I say with the benefit of hindsight and the way my life has developed since. Firstly, I must make clear that I have rejected organised religion in all its forms and hold no regrets on that score. Some may say I am being pretentious when I voice my concerns and sadness for individuals who live their life on the sole basis of religious observance. But that Roman Catholic doctrine of confessing and being forgiven, while controversial with other Christians, did start me of on a process which in a sense continues to this day. I take stock. I try to develop as a human being. I strive for spiritual progress, not in a religious or godly sense, but in expanding my mind and fulfilling myself. I do not do it for self vanity or to puff myself up - for all vanity is like chasing after the wind. Nor am I attempting to build up my portfolio of shares in the so-called after-life. I can, of course, only speak for myself, but I believe I embarked on a journey of beginning to make myself a whole person. In that respect it has been a good thing; a beneficial experience - a thing of beauty and truth.

John Barleycorn

I saw his eyes, his hooded eyes, so distant and so dim,
The very eyes his mother saw as she suckled him.
I watched him as he bedded down - his whole life in a box,
He took the money from his coat and stuffed it in his socks.
Matted hair, bushy beard, a nauseating smell,
I looked into his hooded eyes and asked for him to tell
The story of his life to me, and how from grace he fell.

Those hooded eyes looked back at me, he motioned 'tho to say,
"Come on in to my grand abode, right here in this doorway."
He lit the butt of a cigarette and told to me his name,
"John Barleycorn from Anytown - you and me's the same."
He told me things about myself I didn't know I'd done,
He said he knew about me - that him and I were one.
And someplace in another life, he'd been someone's son.

His hooded eyes became tired as he vividly recalled
How his life was full of love 'till Barleycorn had called,
"I came here many years ago to see if it was true
If all the streets were paved with gold; just the same as you.
And I know all about you - John Barleycorn's your name,
In every horror of our lives 'tis Barleycorn to blame
And you know all about me - you and me's the same."

His hooded eyes closed over into a foggy sleep

So I left him there, in his grand abode, memories to keep.

But in my warm apartment, I failed to close my eyes

As I wondered how in such despair a human soul survives.

When daybreak came next morning, I ventured to the place

Where he had been the night before, to find an empty space.

I thought of what he'd told me and how he fell from grace.

I walked to Cardboard City and there I was informed

My friend had died that winter's night - a victim of Barleycorn.

That frosty night I made my way again

To the grand abode the doorway, which once had housed my friend.

In his place another man was lying just like him

And I saw his eyes, his hooded eyes, so distant and so dim.

He lit the butt of a cigarette and told to me his name,

"John Barleycorn from Anytown - you and me's the same

In every horror of our lives 'tis Barleycorn to blame."

Ma Advice

Keep baith hauns on yer ha'penny an' ye'll no' go very wrong

Whistle if ye must but if ye cannae sing a song

Mind an' haud yer watter if a secret ye are told

An' always keep yer fivers flat; they get weaker wi' the fold

Never build yer hoose on sand, an' dry between yer toes

Be careful on the dodgems if ye're ever at the shows

Always clean the lavvy seat afore ye do the biz

An' watch ye don't inhale before ye eat a Sherbet Fizz

Don't hide yer light beneath a bush; an' keep the doc away

By munchin' on a Granny Smith, each and every day

Look after all yer pennies and yer pounds will be alright

Get up early in the mornin' be in bed before late at night

Cleanliness is next tae Godliness, training keeps ye firm

A bird in yer hand is a lovely thing, but the early wan catches the worm

An' time waits fur no man, no matter who it is

An' always wipe yer arse up the way or ye'll end up lookin' like this!

The Long Sleep

A deadening chill imitated the air
'Though not for the cause of weather
Ma mystified, clasping a rosary
Confused by the rigour or her lament.

Stubborn death had come and gone
Thief-like in night's darkness
Papa lay cold as ice
Mellow in the lingering drama.

Ma virtuously brittle yet resolute
Her dear companion detached
Her conation removed by plunder;
A corsair demanding restitution.

Reprisal for living pawned to mankind
Papa, wayworn and yet liberated
In this transient life, essence complete
Time for it all to end?

ACKNOWLEDGEMENTS

Men with Pens would like to thank the following people:

Awards for All and Scottish Arts Council.

Adam Tierney – Adult Literacy & Numeracy Development Worker

Alexander J. Cunningham

Jim Graham

Tommy McBride

Margaret and William McLean

Andrew Hay

North Lanarkshire Council (Learning & Leisure Services)

Community Learning & Development (Airdrie Locality)

Men with Pens are based in Chapelside Centre, Waddell Street, Airdrie ML6 6JU

All correspondence should be sent to the secretary at the above address.

e-mail: menwithpens@hotmail.co.uk

website address: www.menwithpens.com